Planning, Politics, and the Public Interest

PLANNING, POLITICS, and the PUBLIC INTEREST

EDITED BY
WALTER GOLDSTEIN

NEW YORK   COLUMBIA UNIVERSITY PRESS   1978

Walter Goldstein is professor of political science
at the State University of New York, Albany,
and chairman of the Columbia University Seminar on
Technology and Social Change.

Library of Congress Cataloging in Publication Data
Main entry under title:

Planning, politics, and the public interest.

Includes bibliographical references.
1. United States—Economic policy—1971–
—Addresses, essays, lectures.   I. Goldstein, Walter,
1930–
HC106.7.P58   338.973   78-1720
ISBN 0-231-04538-7

Columbia University Press
New York and Guildford, Surrey

Copyright © 1978 Columbia University Press
Printed in the United States of America

For Batya
and about time

FOREWORD

THE PAPERS AND DISCUSSIONS in this volume reflect the joint interest of the Columbia University Seminar on Technology and Social Change and a major U.S. corporation in current trends in business–government relations. Although the general theme is national planning, the role of government in a private enterprise economy is explored from many points of view. Interest is sharpened by the fact that the corporate participants in the discussions are senior officials of the largest publicly regulated enterprise in the country, the American Telephone and Telegraph Company.

Under the guidance of its versatile chairman, Dr. Walter Goldstein, the Seminar on Technology and Social Change is engaged in a broad-gauged study of government policies where technology plays a vital role. The members of the Seminar, drawn from the faculties at Columbia University and elsewhere, as well as from leading industries and research centers, meet regularly at Columbia University to listen to and discuss papers delivered by invited authorities. Periodically the Seminar participates in conferences such as the one which has resulted in the present book.

Aside from providing a stimulating intellectual experience for the participants, the conference which has produced the papers and discussions recorded in the following chapters illustrates the importance of the University Seminar concept, namely, the study of problems in depth from the varying perspectives of experts drawn from differing, but related, fields of interest. It is our hope that these papers and discussions will prove to be of interest to those concerned with policy-making and analysis in areas affecting the performance of our economy.

Aaron W. Warner,
Director of Columbia University
Seminars

CONTENTS

Introduction   Walter Goldstein   *1*

The New Rationality: The Clash Between the Corporate
and the Public Sector Conceptions of the National
Interest   Andrew Hacker   *10*

Manpower Planning in a Pluralist Economy   Eli Ginzberg   *28*

The Second Managerial Revolution: The Shift of Economic
Decision-Making from Business to Government
Murray L. Weidenbaum   *45*

National Planning and the Multinational Enterprise: The
U.S. Case   Raymond Vernon   *77*

Technological Innovation for the U.S. Civilian Economy:
The Role of Government   Franklin A. Long   *106*

The Inevitability of Planning   Robert Lekachman   *143*

A Response: Planning—Yes, But by Whom?
Gordon T. Bowden   *161*

The Politics of Planning for the Public Interest: The Role of
Liberal Ideology in a Conservative Society
Walter Goldstein   *181*

Appendix: List of Conference Participants   *201*

Planning, Politics, and the Public Interest

INTRODUCTION

WALTER GOLDSTEIN

AMERCIAN POLITICAL LIFE presents a striking paradox: "Planning" is everywhere reviled and everywhere pursued. Corporate managements protest on business grounds against the bureaucratic expansion of planning activities but their own companies hire costly staff to develop sophisticated, long-term plans. Both political parties appeal to the electorate to curb the planning powers of government, but on winning office they insist upon enlarging the legal range and the budgetary expense of government regulation. Economists theorize over the benefits of free market competition, yet many work for regulatory agencies that are charged with protecting major industries against competition. The parodox would be merely ironic had it not come to confuse political debate and economic analysis.

At the core of the confusion is an overlap of ideological and pragmatic values. Conservatives tend to associate planning with socialist ideology and collectivist controls, but liberals identify it with systems analysis, cost-benefit forecasting, and operations research. There is a widespread assumption that planning activities differ in form between the public and the private sectors, but the alleged dichotomy is false. Among private industries, the airlines, utilities, banks, and telecommunication companies have lobbied to preserve administered pricing and public limitations to market entry; while in the public sector, the Departments of Defense and the Interior have claimed that their performance budgeting or price sensitivities are superior to those found among corporate industry. Planning, it seems, has become an expert technology concealed behind a credo of political skepticism.

It was a Nobel laureate in economics, Wassily Leontief, who suggested that planning will be accepted in the American economy when its cause is urged by business leaders rather than by radical activists. The remark should not be taken lightly. Leontief argued that a mechanism as complex and wealthy as the business civilization of America could not survive, in practice, by clinging to the laissez-faire nostrums of a free market ideology. That a truly free market ever existed, in a long-past age of idyllic capitalism, doubted by most historians. Today neither oil millionaires nor scions of the stock exchange yearn to revive the economic struggles or the anarchic competition that were once associated with an open and unregulated economy.

The growing divergence between the folklore and the reality of American capitalism has left a trail of confusion in the political process. The evils of big government are denounced by industrial and political leaders when an election draws near. When they gain office, however, conservative Presidents and Congressmen are as likely to add to the infrastructure of regulatory instruments and bureaucratic controls as were their liberal predecessors. Both political parties strive to recruit executive talent from agribusiness, from banks and industrial conglomerates in order to improve the public sector's management of the economy. Ideological rhetoric has been put aside. Partisan attempts to dismember the apparatus of control have been condemned as dangerous threats to the stability of American business—if only in fact rather than in theory.

The basic disagreements between the advocates of planning and of entrepreneurial freedom are difficult to categorize. No one is quite sure whether the exercises of planning, as we know them, are designed to curb or to preserve the economic system. The managers of vast industrial enterprises take pride in their ability to plan corporate investment schedules and to manage their computerized control instruments. They argue that government regulation is appropriate to limit competition but not to create new social priorities. Financial leaders urge a sharper curb on monetary inflation and a reduction of unemployment levels; but they can not identify anyone, other than government planners, who can fine-tune the controls maintained by federal and state authorities. A little planning is acceptable, it appears, so long as it does not become too effective and so long as its merits do not have to be publicly acknowledged. The current impasse over the formulation of a national energy policy demonstrates our confusion. The oil companies and the President are both criticized for playing the role that is expected of them: they were always expected to scheme, resist, and struggle to define an urgent public interest—but not with an excess of zeal.

A comparable conclusion has been reached in many institutional forums, ranging from local chambers of commerce to the committees of Congress. The house organs of business and labor plead for a more sensitive use of planning instruments but not for their elimination. There are widespread demands for planning to be exercised when resources become scarce, when basic industries falter, or when competition threatens powerful interests. Decisions to allocate natural gas, to protect the steel industry, or to police the banks command broad support among the leaders of business and political parties. Yet the advocacy of public sector planning continues to generate a storm of protest and angry debate when the issues are articulated in public.

It is commonly agreed that the U.S. economy is entering an era of austerity and hardship. The cost of energy has increased fivefold, a recurring deficit has appeared in the balance of payments, and the perils of inflation are permanently factored into our national assessments. That economic resources must be husbanded and social dislocation minimized is clearly apparent. So, too, is the conclusion that society must resort to effective forcasting and program planning if the economy is to improve its capacity for dynamic growth.

It is the division of power in the formulation of plans and forecasts that remains the subject of relentless dispute. Partisans of public or private sector controls remain divided on every issue, except the fundamental one: that *someone* has to exercise planning authority if we are to enjoy a better and a more equitable standard of living.

Identifying the Issues

It was to clarify these important policy disagreements that a conference was called by the University Seminar on Technology and Social Change, which has met at Columbia University since 1962. The conference was joined by senior management from the American Telephone

and Telegraph Company (AT&T). A dozen of their corporate staff met
for a weekend of concentrated and carefully prepared discussion with a
dozen academics who were members or guests of the Seminar. AT&T
generously helped finance the meeting and this publication. Its management exercised no influence, however, in determining which papers
should be presented or what course the discussion should follow. It was
simply agreed that the management and the academic participants,
alike, should avoid scoring debating points as a substitute for a serious
intellectual exchange.

The conference met at Glen Cove on Long Island as the 1976 presidential election campaign moved toward its close. Everyone was sure
that a new era of political action would commence in Washington as the
economy began to recover from the recession of 1975 and 1976. Considerable anxiety was voiced about the nation's economic vigor and its capacity to overcome the challenges that were likely to appear in the late
1970s. It was on the issue of *who should control future growth* that the
conference was strongly divided. The pages of discussion following each
major presentation in this book reveal the critical and opposing arguments that were articulated.

In its first fifteen years the University Seminar tried to respond to the
economic and technological challenges that appeared in the 1960s. Its
success can be measured in the four books that it published with the
Columbia University Press. The first three volumes reflected the spirit
of optimism and innovation that accompanied the rapid growth in federal funding for science efforts and research and development (R&D)
programs in the 1960s. Indeed, many authors in those collections of
papers became distinguished spokesmen for (or critics of) the government's support of big science.[1]

In subsequent years, the seminar reflected the skepticism about government science funding that intensified as the Vietnam war continued
to escalate, as protest movements gathered on the Columbia campus,
and as debate polarized over the role played by NASA, the Defense
Department, and corporate R&D in American universities. The intellectual definition of this skepticism was captured in a fourth book contain-

[1] Eli Ginzberg, ed., *Technology and Social Change* (1964); Aaron W. Warner, Dean
Morse, and Alfred S. Eichner, eds., *The Impact of Science and Technology* (1965); Dean
Morse and Aaron W. Warner, eds., *Technological Innovation and Society* (1969).

ing the papers presented to two conferences jointly sponsored with *Time* magazine.[2] The contributors included Sir Isaiah Berlin, I. I. Rabi, Jacob Bronowski, David Sidorsky, Eli Ginzberg, and Loren Eiseley.

Among the unique activities at Columbia University are the specialized seminars that meet each month during the academic year. Seventy-four different seminars are in continuous session. Their concerns range from the Renaissance or cultural pluralism to oriental thought, Latin America, contemporary Africa, and the history of the working class. Nearly 3,000 members attend the monthly meetings; they are drawn from Columbia and other university faculties, from Washington agencies, the United Nations, the labor movement, the mass media, and corporate business. The discussions have enriched the intellectual life of New York, and a considerable number of seminar papers have been published in academic monographs and journals.

The decision to publish a fifth book for the Seminar on Technology and Social Change was warmly supported both by Columbia University and AT&T. AT&T had just completed a centennial review of its performance in cooperation with faculty at the Massachusetts Institute of Technology.[3] It was proposed that a conference should review the contemporary meaning of political planning and resource allocation in the American economy. The Seminar and the Bell System welcomed the idea and resolved that the project should be pursued in a nonpolemical, analytical mode. The success of the project can be gauged in the papers that were produced and in the edited record of the discussion that followed each presentation. The responsibility for editing the recording tapes lies solely with the chairman of the Seminar, though all participants were asked to review an earlier draft of the discussion pages.

The first paper, prepared by Andrew Hacker, formulates a unique approach to the subject of public versus private sector planning. As a political scientist and social historian, Hacker perceives a "new rationality" intruding into American society. It is not antibusiness, radical, egalitarian, or profoundly philosophical, but it does question the commercial

[2] Aaron W. Warner, Dean Morse, and Thomas E. Cooney, eds., *The Environment of Change* (1969).

[3] The first books to appear were *The Telephone's First Century—and Beyond* (New York: Crowell, 1976), and Ithiel de Sola Pool, ed., *The Social Impact of the Telephone* (Cambridge: M.I.T. Press, 1977).

truthfulness and the social expectations of corporate business. There is a
pervasive skepticism, he argues, that reflects the disenchantment of a
consumer society that is employed, fed, and clothed by business organizations. Holding that liberalism and conservatism are obsolete ideologies
for our planless society, Hacker observes a mounting dissatisfaction with
the performance of corporate management among an educated and affluent electorate.

Drawing upon his extensive research and government experience in
manpower policy, Eli Ginzberg is skeptical about economic planning for
a different set of reasons. Manpower and employment practices are not
as susceptible to accurate measurement and control as many theorists
tend to argue, nor are the techniques of government as sophisticated as
advocates of central planning might imagine. Both government and business lack the data needed to establish a realistic information base. The
demographic profile of the work force is subtly shaded and constantly
changing; social reformers, government economists, and business managers must therefore tread cautiously when they decide to change the
definition of welfare standards or of minimum wage rates. A shocking
waste of human resources persists in our society. Moreover, the dearth
of meaningful work is likely to increase the level of injury and dislocation in the years ahead. If the worst consequences of underemployment
and youthful unemployment are to be avoided, manpower planning
must be flexible and innovative. It must defy rigid theorizing from the
Left and the Right, and it must focus upon the plight of the hidden, the
permanent, and the job-hungry communities of the poor.

This emphasis upon public needs moves the next author to a different
conclusion. As a former Assistant Secretary of the Treasury, Murray
Weidenbaum finds compelling reasons to doubt the efficacy of government regulation and planning, no matter how good the intentions might
be. The increased cost of complying with regulatory codes has come to
inhibit the entrepreneurial vigor of industry and to saddle it with appall-
ing bureaucratic constraints. He insists that a "second managerial revolution" has taken place in recent years. A silent transfer of power has
curtailed the profit-seeking authority of private enterprise and expanded
the regulatory interventions of insensitive public agencies. If the process
is not halted or reversed, Weidenbaum warns, there will be a serious

erosion in the competitive prowess and the productive performance of American business.

Attention is drawn to the problems of national planning and the control of international trade by Raymond Vernon. The founder of the Multinational Enterprises Project at the Harvard Business School, Vernon notes that national planning has usually stopped at the frontier post; it rarely intervenes in the critical trade flows within the international economy. Although planning forms vary greatly among leading industrial states, few governments have chosen to deflect or to inhibit the global movement of capital, trade, or industrial transfers. A few states have tried to protect their weaker industries or to spur the development of their domestic economy. When it comes to tangling with multinational enterprises and banks, however, the ambitions of state planning have been muted. The movement patterns in the international economy are too elusive to be constrained, in a profitable manner, by protectionist or *dirigiste* controls.

The limitations of national planning are regarded in a different light by Franklin Long. As an academic who has served in senior positions in both government and industry, Long remains surprised by the information that has *not* been gathered by the public and private sectors. Spending nearly $40 billion a year on R&D, government and corporate management have failed to calculate the input/output ratios generated by major science programs. The productivity of technological investments in military, space, commercial, and international programs is difficult to measure. Until some reliable gauge of cost-effective funding is developed, it will be difficult to devise a national plan to allocate R&D expenditures or to chart the science priorities that should receive preferential funding in an economy aiming for systematic growth.

The discussion takes a sharp turn in the last two papers. Robert Lekachman, an economist who has written trenchantly about Keynesian theory and current political problems, asserts not only that planning is pervasive in the contemporary economy but that its future growth is inevitable. Although American politics does not have an active Left to mobilize political support for collectivist planning, Lekachman finds that more and more businessmen have come to recognize the benefits that regulatory planning can bring to the advancement of national wealth.

Economic development can no longer proceed in a haphazard or a lack-luster manner; nor can it be retarded by the scarcities (of energy or employment) that are likely to emerge in the next few years. Lekachman suggests that political activism will rise again, as it did in the New Deal era, if only to guarantee the survival of the capitalist system. Coopera-tion between the public and private sectors will be welcomed so that the wastage of resources and the wasted utilization of human skills can be curbed. It is the business managers rather than the politicians who have appreciated this apparently novel idea. Many of them, Lekachman re-ports, have already begun to translate their newly found heresies into respectable action programs.

As chairman of the conference, Walter Goldstein had to defer the presentation of his own position. In a paper written after the session he focuses on a problem that requires further analysis: the redistribution of economic power in a politically pluralist system. Pluralist theory as-sumes that "the public interest" can be realistically defined through in-tergroup bargaining and partial gains, but he finds serious shortcomings in a society dominated by business values and corporate organization. If planning is to lead to effective policy control, he argues, there will have to be a certain amount of pain in the transfer of power from the private to the public management of the economy. Should the leaders of politi-cal groups shrink from inflicting such pain, while continuing to toy with partial and pragmatic compromises, the debate over policy planning will remain an exercise in shadow boxing. Economic planning will never be a significant issue in American politics unless a decision is made to sys-tematically redistribute wealth, privilege, and authority in a society con-demned to slow growth. There is no sign that the debate over planning is about to move in this direction. Hence the issues involved are not heated, but they are gently obscured by rhetoric and diversion.

The discussion following the first six presentations was lively and productive. An attempt has been made to summarize the arguments that were made by the twenty-six invited participants.[4] Considerable editing

[4] Apart from the conference participants, whose names and affiliations are listed in the Appendix, I would like to acknowledge the valuable assistance provided by three other persons: Batya Goldstein, who handled all of the tape recording and conference arrange-ments, and Maria Caliandro, who edited the manuscript with great care and saw it through production for Columbia University Press; and especially Bill Bowden, Director of Educa-

has been done to clarify the main themes in the debate and to contrast the divergent positions adopted in each discussion.

No grand conclusions can be announced in a symposium of this order, but there is a revealing juxtaposition of assumptions, challenges, and policy judgments. The purpose of the conference was to pit one set of ideas against another and to examine one of the most serious but confusing debates of the present time. Whatever were the failures in our analysis of planning, politics, and the public interest, each of the participants left the conference with a new range of doubts, insights, and curiosities. This is the only objective for which a seminar or an academic symposium can strive. The hope is that this structured analysis will contribute to the contemporary literature on economic planning.

tional Relations in the Public Relations and Employee Information Department at AT&T, who provided generous assistance at each stage of the planning and execution of this project.

THE NEW RATIONALITY

The Clash Between the Corporate and the Public Sector Conceptions of the National Interest

ANDREW HACKER

FOR THE NEXT SEVERAL YEARS at least, business will be burdened with
new kinds and qualities of regulation. Increasingly, its activities will
have to comply with rules ranging from health and safety, through discrimination and disclosure, to protection of the environment and consultation with local communities. Murray Weidenbaum's paper will
consider official intervention in this sphere. By the same token, there
will be more talk of economic planning as an ongoing obligation of government. Such proposals, often coming from respectable quarters,
would conform business behavior to public projections on such matters
as employment, inflation, and even income distribution. Robert Lekachman's essay will proffer such a forecast.

My paper has a more preliminary purpose. It is intended to shed light

Andrew Hacker is professor of political science at Queens College of the City University
of New York.

on current sources of support for both government regulation of business and moves toward economic planning. The past generation has brought important changes to our major social parameters. In particular, people have new outlooks and occupations, new expectations and ideologies. The analysis that follows will focus on a complex of ideas I call "the New Rationality." I shall argue that this mode of thought is the chief cause of the discomforts presently besetting business. But first, a few words on how we conceived of ourselves in the past.

It is fitting, in this bicentennial year, to remember that America began as a business society. As it happens, we have become rather diffident about these origins. Hence the stress on the purely political side of our beginnings, as expressed in the Declaration of Independence, the Constitution, and the Bill of Rights. Yet that period produced another, less heralded, manifesto setting forth assumptions on which this nation was founded. Its author was Alexander Hamilton, our original Secretary of the Treasury. His "Report on the Subject of Manufactures," submitted toward the end of 1791, declared independence for productive property, sketched out an economic constitution, and affirmed the basic rights of entrepreneurship.

And like all manifestos, its message rose as much from its spirit as from its substance. Hamilton was essentially a romantic. For him, business was a great adventure, a calling wherein individuals might express their truest creative talents. Two typical paragraphs show how Hamilton's vision involved much more than production and profits. He wanted Americans to become energetic, imaginative, inspired. Only in a business society, he argued, would citizens reach the pinnacles of which they are capable:

It is a just observation that the minds of the strongest and most active powers fall below mediocrity, and labor without effect, if confined to uncongenial pursuits. And it is thence to be inferred that the results of human exertion may be immensely increased by diversifying its objects. When all the different kinds of industry obtain in a community, each individual can find his proper element and can call into activity the whole vigor of his nature. . . .

To cherish and stimulate the activity of the human mind, by multiplying the objects of enterprise, is not among the least considerable of the expedients by which the wealth of a nation may be promoted. Even things in themselves not positively advantageous sometimes become so

by their tendency to provoke exertion. Every new scene which is
opened to the busy nature of man to rouse and exert itself is the addition
of a new energy to the general stock of effort.[1]

And the country rose to that challenge. Armadas of immigrants arrived on our shores, knowing that in America property was both re-
spected and easily acquired. (Nor should we forget that with America's
system of land tenure, the family farm became a business enterprise.)
Citizens were encouraged to launch their own endeavors and imprint
their personalities on them. No one frowned on commercial ingenuity or
material accumulation. It was the American way. Instead of honoring
generals, we made heroes of Henry Ford, Thomas Edison, and Alexander Graham Bell. (Note, too, that these men were not only inventors.
They also participated in the business sides of their discoveries.)

Our captains were of industry. What were the achievements of a Ben-
jamin Harrison, a William Howard Taft, even a Theodore Roosevelt,
compared with those of our Carnegies and Rockefellers, an Alfred Sloan,
or a Theodore Vail? And like Hamilton, they were unabashed romantics.
For them, the nation was a raw Mount Rushmore, on which they would
carve memorials to themselves. In a word, they made capitalism work.
And in the process, they created an economy that was the envy of the
world. As stated in one of the best-known celebrations of that system,
they "accomplished wonders far surpassing Egyptian pyramids, Roman
aqueducts, and Gothic cathedrals."[2] No small compliment, this, for
United States Steel, Standard Oil, and a privately held telecommunications system.

Such an economy is inherently anarchic. Of course laissez-faire has
always had its limits, many sponsored by businessmen themselves. Even
so, in America just about anyone with ambition and access to some capital can come up with a product or service and attempt to sell it to some-
body else. Indeed, what we built was less a "system" than a grandiose
medieval fair: a cacophony of sales and deals, fueled by greed and envy
plus a measure of subliminal sex. Its methods were extraordinarily
wasteful, and have usually been slippery with the facts. At least half of

[1] Alexander Hamilton, "Report on the Subject of Manufactures," in *Papers on Public
Credit, Commerce, and Finance* (Indianapolis: Bobbs-Merrill, 1957), pp. 195, 196.
[2] Karl Marx and Friedrich Engels, *Communist Manifesto*, in *Selected Works* (Moscow:
Foreign Languages Publishing House, n.d.), vol. I, p. 37.

all products made, bought, and sold are not "needed" by any objective reckoning. Much of our economic life is largely frivolous.

Business success goes to those who have a hunch for what other people want, those who sense how history will be moving. If we wish to have rising living standards, and a varied and entertaining life, then economic anarchy is surely the best route. "Multiplying the objects of enterprise," said Hamilton, "is . . . among . . . the expedients by which the wealth of a nation may be promoted." In so saying, he converted his countrymen into followers of Adam Smith—whose bicentennial we have strangely neglected.

The modern corporation is heir to this tradition. Even with its information systems, professionalized managements, and multigenerational computers, business remains on its rendezvous with romance. It is still trying to sell us things we don't actually need, even items we don't want. For all the burning issues of the day—an international energy crisis, world overpopulation, the breakdown of the nuclear family—it is nice to know that someone out there thinks that each of us ought to have a Trimline telephone.

Every economic development sows seeds that will later torment it. In America's case, Hamilton also described these antithetical embryos. Ours was to be a highly mechanized economy, with productivity its guiding principle. "The employment of machinery," he explained, "is an artificial force brought in aid of the natural force of man." (All this had to be spelled out simply, for his agriculturally oriented colleagues.) Machines, he went on, constitute "an increase of hands, an accession of strength, unencumbered too by the expense of maintaining the laborer." Hence he posed a question, to which he obviously knew the answer:

May it not, therefore, be fairly inferred, that those occupations which give greatest scope to the use of this auxiliary contribute most to the general stock of industrious effort, and, in consequence, to the general product of industry?[3]

We should take heed of Hamilton's emphasis: it is on *occupations* that will heighten productivity. What he had in mind, as much as anything, was an economy willing to make use of its engineers—a profession dedi-

[3] Hamilton, "Report on Manufacturers," p. 192.

cated to securing the greatest possible number of outputs from the fewest feasible inputs.

Here, too, Hamilton's vision became the reality. Accompanying our entrepreneurial adventurers were inventors and improvers, men with stopwatches and slide rules, calipers and graph paper. In time came industrial laboratories, subsidized universities, and a vocation—if not a religion—called "research." These activities, first seen as handservants of commerce, would soon prove themselves at war with their progenitor.

One example shows how this process can work. Examine the experience of a physicist named William Shockley, employed by the Bell Telephone Laboratories. How was he to know that his simple industrial innovation would mature to transform the organization he so faithfully served? His transistor, more than any other single instrument, revolutionized our modes of production. It took people out of fields and factories, and placed them in offices and classrooms. It gave them time to talk and the leisure to think. In alliance with its offspring, the computer and the integrated circuit, it produced new structures of logic, new languages of symbols and numeration. Within a single generation, everyone would come under its sway. Even those who pride themselves on their distance from technology are affected more than they know. (The very beat of electronic rock'n'roll shapes categories and cadences of perception.)

Industrial efficiency means that an economy can reach high living standards with a relatively modest labor force. Given the central role of machines (not to mention lasers, petrochemicals, and assorted polymers), industry would have no need for everyone's services. Our success in the sphere of productivity brought a host of unforeseen consequences.

For one thing, we have created a new lumpenproletariat of people for whom the economy has no use whatever. These are superfluous human beings, who provide no discernible service apart from allowing the rest of us to feel superior. The application of rationality to industry has thus created an entire class of human beings victimized by the system's own logic. Their very presence cannot help but be a commentary on such an economy's incapacity for absorbing all of its human assets. And this inability in turn raises questions about the contours of industrial rationality. How can so sublime a technological creation tolerate so much human havoc? Not a few citizens begin to sense a basic contradiction between the rationality of our latest inventions and the irrationality of an economy unable to integrate so much of its population. More than that, the awareness of these contradictions arises out of perceptions brought into being by modern technology.

There is another side to the employment picture. With industry not needing everyone, more and more people could postpone their entry into employment. Indeed, with our technology so productive, cash became increasingly available for pleasant pursuits like higher education. Thus a growing segment of Americans could spend enjoyable interludes in classrooms, on campuses, in congenial company and conversation. In the quarter-century from 1950 to 1974, the proportion of Americans aged 25 and older attending college almost doubled, rising from 13 percent to 25 percent. Among individuals aged 25 to 35, no less than 20 percent currently hold college diplomas. It would be too much to call these people a new leisure class. After all, most eventually end up on a payroll. Even so, such a prolonged exemption from employment affects their ideology and personality. And on the whole, these effects are not helpful for business.

For example, we have seen a pandemic rise in professionalism. Education is largely responsible for this. Given the availability of attractive credentials, it is understandable that people will want to become economists and agronomists, journalists and psychiatrists, accountants and chemists—indeed, almost anything in preference to being businessmen. Put simply, the United States has far fewer people today who regard themselves as belonging to the business community. As a result, the constituency for business values grows smaller with each passing year.

A glance at some census returns shows the amplitude of these shifts. In 1950, the country had only 4.5 million persons prepared to describe themselves as professionals, compared with 10.1 million who were salespeople or members of management. Under this ratio, people in business occupations outnumbered professionals by a margin of 2.2 to 1. By 1975, the work force contained close to 13 million professionals, only slightly short of the 14.1 million salespeople and managers. Now businessmen and women outnumber professionals by a mere 1.1 to 1. Looking at the same statistics from a different angle, sales and managerial personnel rose by only 38 percent over this 25-year period, less than the rise for the work force as a whole. In contrast, professional employment increased by almost 200 percent, more than four times the figure for the work force.

Moreover, many of our current "managers" are employed in government agencies or private nonprofit organizations, such as hospitals, institutes, and foundations—archetypes of Eli Ginzberg's "pluralist economy." Statistics for some specific occupations illuminate the overall picture. Between the 1950 and 1970 censuses, while the work force grew by 37 percent, the number of journalists rose by 61 percent, the ranks of social workers swelled by 184 percent, and college professors ballooned by 287 percent. In addition, among people who called themselves "managers" back in 1950, almost 60 percent were self-employed. By the 1970 census, fewer than 25 percent of all managers ran their own enterprises; the rest, the vast majority, were now on someone else's payroll.

If these figures have a fairly familiar ring, what is less well understood is how these new modes of employment have shaped attitudes toward business activities. Let me offer some speculations on this subject.

We hear much of how ideology has declined in this country. "Liberalism" and "conservatism" are obsolete or ambiguous or irrelevant. Or so we are told. And in large measure this analysis is correct. Very few people are willing to affix labels to themselves or identify with specifiable viewpoints. We have many more self-styled "moderates" and "independents" than either liberals or conservatives or radicals. And even among those accepting such designations, attitudes are usually ambivalent or overlapping. People obviously have all sorts of opinions about what is happening in the world around them. Even so, those sentiments lack coherent expression. Put another way, very few Americans have a "world view" into which they can key all of their attitudes. Nor is this surprising. There is no law which says that we will always be able to come up with ideas suitable for the circumstances of our period. We may tell ourselves that we "need" such thinking. But that does not mean we will get it. Not every age can conjure up a Locke or a Rousseau. In fact, most never do.

All this said, I will argue that there is an ideology in the air at this time, even if its adherents are largely unaware of it. This is the thinking

I have alluded to as the New Rationality. And I use this phrase largely because I wish to link the mode of thought with the technological and organizational processes which brought it on the scene.

Yet let me stress here and now that most proponents of the New Rationality do not think of themselves as liberals, socialists, radicals, or even intellectuals. Most are quite typical middle-class Americans: moderately educated homeowners who complain about taxes, enjoy their material comforts, and occasionally watch "Masterpiece Theatre." They are not overly anxious to share the things they have achieved, although they would deny that they are selfish. For instance, they prefer to put some distance between themselves and society's problem people. We don't find them volunteering their children to improve school-integration statistics, nor do they petition to have public housing on their block.

What I am saying, then, is that the New Rationality is not really redistributive. In that sense, it differs from ideologies expressed by the New Deal and the Great Society. It has given up on warring against poverty, bussing schoolchildren, and soaking the rich. To put the matter in succinct (if oversimple) terms, its concern is less with redressing injustice than with reducing the chaos of our society. What the New Rationality wants is a more sensible social and economic order. And it wishes to use governmental agencies to achieve that end.

We are familiar enough with the cases. I cite several here, but merely to establish the context. There is, for instance, the new obsession with the environment. The New Rationality has rediscovered the order of nature, with industry cast as its mortal adversary. Upon learning that Allied Industries intends to build a new plant, the first question concerns how the raising of that installation will affect the grebe and the grackle.

For better and for worse, our economy was built by freebooters who took a predatory attitude toward the environment. Rivers, forests, and the atmosphere were to be used rather than revered. The New Rationality would have our third century give ecology its first priority. Under this regimen, business corporations would become compliant creatures, ready to defer to the flora and fauna. The outcome would be an economy in which not much might get produced; but what did would be exceedingly virtuous.

A further example of the New Rationality lies in the support for full disclosure, truth in advertising, and labels telling the whole story. In our earlier experience of capitalism, consumership was also an adventure. Advertisers felt free to engage in hyperbole, promising far more than their products could deliver. Buyers learned how to be skeptical, discounting sales pitches by at least 80 percent. The economic arena was a battle of wits. Moreover, it did wonders for our sense of humor. (It is no accident that our strongest commercial traditions—the Yankee trader and the Jewish peddler—produced the country's foremost comedians. I urge Marxist scholars looking for dissertation topics to consider the economic origins of humor.)

The New Rationality stands in mortal fear that some consumer, somewhere, may succumb to the side effects of a mislabeled mayonnaise. The day will soon come when advertising for a perfume called *Eros* will have to include a disclaimer that the people in the picture aren't actually in love, but are merely simulating affection for a fee. Even now, commercials feel obliged to include a voice-over admitting that she would probably have gotten him even had she not switched to Ultra-Dent. (After all, might not some hapless user sue the company, complaining that the product failed to deliver on its promise?)

Truth is clearly central to the New Rationality. And if we want a truthful economy, we should understand that it comes at a price. For this emphasis on veracity is new. Traditionally, capitalism has called for at least a measure of prevarication—if only to induce people to buy those things they don't particularly need, don't want, and probably can't afford anyway. The more truth we have, the less people will buy on impulse. And that is bound to have consequences for the economy. The facts are fine in their place. But they are not the best of means for ensuring full employment.

From installing seatbelts to monitoring children's television to stopping supersonics—in each case the New Rationality supersedes sales, expansion, and profits. Every society is entitled to set its moral and cultural priorities. But let us not complain when our lights flicker a bit and we pay more for cars spewing fewer emissions. If a nation makes certain choices, it should be mature enough to live with their consequences.

What I have sought to depict here is the growing constituency for what I have called, in my subtitle, "the public sector conception of the national interest." And what I am suggesting is that the rise in public regulation, inspection, and litigation, plus proposals for governmental economic planning, should *not* be attributed to such easy targets as populist politicians, irresponsible intellectuals, empire-building bureaucrats, or opportunist advocates. All these obviously play a role. (It would be silly to deny Ralph Nader's influence.) Even so, the support for the New Rationality comes from a citizenry of growing proportions. And far from being radical, its typical member is as likely as not to be a suburban housewife who reads *Newsweek* and takes her cues from David Brinkley's eyebrow.

Most of all I would like to emphasize that these attitudes stem from forces put into motion by industry itself. Unwittingly, perhaps even unwillingly, the technological revolution of our times has evoked outlooks subversive of the entrepreneurial tradition. "The advance of industry produces above all its own gravediggers."[4] If business can no longer rouse the sympathies it feels it deserves, the fault lies not in poor communications or failing to get its story across. If less of its audience is listening, it is because the thrust of industrial progress has attuned the ears of millions of middle-class Americans to the beat of a different drummer.

[4] Marx and Engels, *Communist Manifesto*, p. 45.

Discussion

The Public Sector and the Public Interest

ELI GINZBERG. I agree with the two basic themes of Andrew Hacker's paper. Our society has been concerned with material goods and productivity and it has succeeded beyond its wildest expectations. Levels of real income, though not well shared, are so substantial that struggling for further increments is less urgent. Some people have enough money to prolong their education, to take long vacations, or to retire early. Even those who are not well off, and whose margins of freedom are constricted, are not starving. In the 1930s I saw people looking in garbage cans for food but I see nothing like that today.

You are also right in saying that we need not look for new ideological propositions to explain contemporary social change. Social behavior has been fundamentally altered. Americans are no longer driven by dire need or by Alexander Hamilton's romantic conception of business when they work for an organization as complex as AT&T. In previous centuries, people worked so that they could accumulate wealth and win a measure of personal freedom. Today we have shifted our priorities. We are less committed to work as a means toward wealth accumulation or to business identification with society.

MURRAY WEIDENBAUM. I would like to enter two disagreements with Andrew Hacker's delightful essay.

First, I am always intrigued by specificity. "40 percent of the products that we consume are not needed." He sounds precise. But we also hear that 40 percent of women cheat on their husbands; and it is equally difficult to verify that proposition.

Second, there is the question of the lumpenproletariat and who is *not* needed in the work force. Here we must calculate the marginal productivity of each worker and whether public policy has priced all too many workers beyond the limits of marginal cost. Teenagers are especially vulnerable to our generous increase of the minimum wage. In raising it, we have greatly increased their unemployment. It is through a misuse of public sector policy, therefore, that we have burdened the productivity of the private sector.

ELI GINZBERG. I really cannot agree. In 1900 we had no minimum-wage laws but there was serious underemployment of youth. There still is today, along with underemployment of millions of blacks and women. As a system, capitalism has never provided work for everyone, whether in the United States or in the European models of a market society. We cannot explain our changing attitudes to work simply because we have adopted reasonable minimum-wage legislation.

JACK KOTEN. Private industry has taken an altogether different view of work than the academic world supposes. In AT&T we have used technology to improve labor efficiency and to control operating expenses more effectively. While this has helped keep rates low for our customers, it has also provoked sharp criticism from regulatory commissions at both the federal and state levels and from labor unions.

Look at this paradox carefully. It has been said that our technological achievements have improved economic efficiency but thwarted the fulfillment of a primary social goal—the expansion of work opportunities. Our objective was not to add to unemployment but to render a less costly service. What is it then that Prof. Hacker has criticized? The private sector's pursuit of industrial efficiency, or the public sector's choice of nonindustrial priorities?

SYLVIA HEWLETT. I find it difficult to maintain this simple distinction between the public and the private sectors, or their diverging responsibilities to provide for full employment. It revives memories of the false promises of the Great Society programs of ten years ago. At that time we confused educational upgrading and manpower training for the individual with overall employment policy. Today we find that 8 or 9 percent unemployment rates are judged as desirable consequences (or not) of macroeconomic policy; but we do not envisage the impact on individual workers, blacks, teenagers, or women.

In Sweden they chose the direct antithesis of our policy. For social

reasons they preferred inflation or an imbalance of payments to the
dread results of underemployment. In an era of costly inflation today,
they continue to do so. The explanation is quite straightforward. There
is a radically different structuring of power relationships in Swedish than
in American society. Their attitudes to the lumpenproletariat and its
work needs are critically different from our own.

ELI GINZBERG. Let me follow up on that particular point, though in a
different direction. Power in our society is diffused through the political
system, but the voting majority, as Andrew Hacker noted, lies with
those who have something to protect. We expect a capitalist economy to
be dynamic but we also expect the regulatory force of government to
protect the vested interests, whether of the many or the few. We must
not dichotomize, therefore, between the efficiency of one sector as
against the welfare of the general public.

Political Conflicts and Economic Values

RAYMOND VERNON. There is one dichotomy that must be emphasized.
The structure and the process of private sector activities must be clearly
distinguished from those in the public realm. It is just not sufficient to
say that commercial organizations are impelled toward growth and stability for the sake of profit, while public agencies are not.

The U.S. political system is conventionally described as a *process* to
diffuse power, to divide authority and distribute influence. Access to
public power can be gained through the committees of Congress, the executive agencies, the courts, or through the new "sunshine laws" (which
among other things compel officials to initiate or to reject a set of
specific official actions).

Moreover, the open and loose-jointed structures of public power differ significantly from the private sector. Several hundred leading
companies in the U.S. economy are managed in a highly predictable
manner by a known cluster of executives. But unlike the situation in
other countries, civil servants in the United States are neither trained
nor socialized to exercise public power. Consequently, their modes of
recruitment and behavior are not predictable.

WALTER GOLDSTEIN. The lack of certainty or prediction in our society
is obviously important. What we call "planning" is markedly different in

the corporate structures of the economy than among the myriad agencies of government. Not only is there a greater certainty in the ratio of input to output in the private sector and a greater stability among the executive cadres involved. There is also an implicit approval for entrepreneurial planning which government bureaucrats do not enjoy.

Government is charged with regulating (and in a few cases, promoting) the competition for scarce economic resources. Federal and state agencies engage in systems forecasting, indicative planning, or coercive regulation, according to their charters. But it is difficult to accept three assumptions that are commonly held: (1) that access to public offices of power is plural and open-ended; (2) that consumers are as likely to be recruited into public management cadres as are representatives of producing companies; and (3) that the cadres, once in office, will question popular interpretations of the "public interest" to the point of undermining the profit axioms of corporate industrial power.

But let me return to the central point at issue: Is planning perceived to be the central activity in the U.S. economy, no matter how it is shared between entrepreneurial and government managers? Is the struggle to plan, as Schumpeter and Galbraith put it, to be seen as a competitive response to technological change; or should we, instead, see the struggle as an ideological combat to accelerate and thus control the pace of economic change?

DAVID APTER. It is worth returning to Andrew Hacker's point that we can no longer retain the originating beliefs of our society. His case is compelling. The public and private marketplaces are neither economically rational nor politically innovative in helping us adjust to the uncertainties of systemic change.

In the past it was assumed, in liberal thought, that market mechanisms would provide adequate opportunities for the development of skills and that scarcity would itself create a thrust toward growth. But what we have found, in practice, is that the force of innovation creates greater scarcities; that the unequal distribution of opportunities generates intolerable uncertainty; and that industrial societies require a complex of planning activities, regardless of their ideological priorities, to cope with the disruptive forces of change.

Albert Hirschman once said that it would be impossible to govern a society that was not product-minded. It would simply not know how to evaluate its own needs and objectives. This relates to the questions that were formulated by Walter Goldstein. Can we identify the prescriptive planning that is actually done, or that should be done, in a society which is confused about its own products and powers? It appears that we have no package of program solutions and no ideological presuppositions to guide us toward system change. But can we devise a product orientation that will, at a minimum, allow us to evaluate the objectives for which we must plan?

Accountability as a Political Reality

DONALD HONICKY. There is one prescriptive element in planning that has been overlooked so far. I refer neither to the motives nor the mechanisms of planning but to the constraints of accountability. In corporate industry we are held closely accountable to our shareholders, to our employees, and above all to the market. In government, given the diffusion of power that has been mentioned, management plans for others to take action—while remaining detached from a direct sense of responsibility.

MARIO SALVADORI. I really cannot accept your statement. As a citizen and as a telephone subscriber, I cannot hold AT&T accountable for its enormous power of decision. I can only threaten to terminate my service; and that will cripple my functioning without even touching you.

ROSALIND SENECA. I must share this criticism but in a different manner. Utility and commercial enterprises were never supposed to provide democratic access for the redress of grievances. I vote at a presidential election, not at the AT&T annual meeting, if I want to secure change in industries' priorities. By applying myself politically I expect the planning powers of the public sector to correct any problems that I find in the private. Obviously, both must work in unison if accountability is to be enforced.

DAVID APTER. At a certain level of complexity, both capitalist and socialist societies find it difficult to institutionalize the full participation of consumers, workers, and managers that is necessary to an efficient mode of planning. The collectivist planning of the Stalin era was a monstrous failure; necks were broken in order to remove obstacles from information feedback channels but the process of industrial adaptation still failed. In our own society, but for very different reasons, corporate industry has also failed to forecast the dimensions of impending change.

We will blind ourselves to a valuable set of alternatives to public and private sector planning, however, if we fail to consider the experience recorded outside the United States. I would like to mention my research findings from interviews that I held with workers in two distant countries, Chile and Yugoslavia.

During the Allende period the Chilean workers were deeply confused about their accountability for public planning. Democratic self-management from the shop floor was a fine abstraction until they discovered that it required hours of their time. The workers wanted to be paid time and a half if they were to work during the day but talk about their work at night. Productivity dropped, unfortunately, as the government tried to rally their efforts to democratize Chilean socialism.

In Yugoslavia the movement for workers' participation has been more successful. It has been designed as a system of socialism from above but capitalism below. Workers on the shop floor have urged each other forward to increase their collective productivity. Our distinction between public and private accountability pales in significance before their complex experiments to harness workers' capitalism to central planning. We should not ignore their innovation, as it is likely to be copied elsewhere in the world.

The Language Of Planning

JACK KOTEN. There is no disagreement that every sector in the economy must plan, given the speed and the uncertainty of technological change, but there is conflict over the goals and motives of planners.

In AT&T we must not only achieve a realistic rate of profit to satisfy our shareholders but we must also conform to certain public expectations. Our policies and rates are subject to the review of numerous rate-setting commissions at the federal and state levels. Furthermore, we must respond to serious, costly, and time-consuming allegations that we have infringed the antitrust laws. With all of this, we are expected to achieve a high degree of operational efficiency.

Recent studies of government operations have revealed ever greater deficiencies in controlling its own programs and balancing its own budgets. AT&T is thus forced into an unenviable position: we are expected by government to do what it can not do, itself. We must safeguard our return on investment. But at the same time we must promote the efficiency of customer services, the speedy introduction of new technology, and the better utilization of societal resources.

WALTER GOLDSTEIN. In short, you have confirmed the point at issue. The private sector has no option but to work with the public if it is to anticipate the momentous changes of our times. If it is to minimize the social costs that we must all pay in the process of adjustment, the private sector must be accessible to public choices.

AT&T has recently placed expensive advertisements in the press to emphasize, in its centennial year, that the Bell System "did not just grow"; it was planned as a system, or as a natural monopoly. AT&T is now arguing before the courts to retain the planning benefits that can only be realized if its monopoly status remains intact. Why is it necessary, therefore, to distrust the less monopolistic planning of the public sector?

Proposed legislation, such as the Humphrey–Javits and Humphrey–Hawkins bills, takes us nowhere close to the Swedish dimensions of planning, but corporate industry has denounced them as a profound threat to our freedom. In fact, these mild proposals would exert a slighter planning impact than many of the decisions reached by AT&T on its own behalf.

JOSEPH MURPHY. Semantics cannot be ignored in this new turn to the discussion. We regard "planning" as an anathema. It suggests creeping socialism, rigid ideological commitments, and the aspirations of Third World regimes to legislate instant collectivism.

We tend to use the terminology of political ideology when we argue about "planning," or we switch to economic metaphors about corporate incentives and profit forecasts. But our language must also allow for the concepts of social and human planning. HEW has developed sensitive indicators of social dislocation, and in the educational system we really believe in minimizing injustice or hardship in our crowded society.

Admittedly, our fitful experience at planning for the War on Poverty was fairly dismal. But we need not retreat, out of linguistic fear, from the reality that we all do plan and expect some of our lives to be

planned. We use social forecasting to estimate our educational or Social Security needs; and we finance counseling services to help young
people plan their careers or their psychological adjustment. Why then
does it induce such anxiety in a business-minded society to admit that
planning is as vital as it is desirable?

Summation

ANDREW HACKER. Let me return to my opening theme. American business was born and flourished in a political ethos of public support. As we
moved from an agrarian to an industrial economy, we maintained the inherent legitimacy of business motives and methods. We still do so.

What we remain unsure about are the planning roles of business enterprise as it anticipates future change. I noted with interest that an
officer of AT&T referred to the revolutionary experiences of planning in
China; and that another referred to the fact that his own children had
begun to question the efficacy of the U.S. business system. It seems that
the questioning of community values is not reserved to academic
theorists.

I used capital letters in writing about the New Rationality as a form of
mock solemnity. In our society we have little faith in extensive public
planning. Nor do we assume that tinkering with capitalism will be very
successful. But I do believe that we are groping in our new rationality
for something other than socialism, radicalism, or collectivism. Between
the theories of Karl Marx and Adam Smith, I side with the latter.

What I envisage is a new constituency that, while it is unwilling to
surrender its basic comforts and privileges, is still going to make life increasingly difficult for corporations like AT&T. Using its newly found rationality to dissociate itself from the business world, it is likely to
exacerbate the tensions between the public and the private sectors.

For my part, I am sure that we will not follow the Chinese or the
Swedish modes of planning. It is likely that the present and the next
generation of the new constituency will persist in the American reliance
on muddle. The conflict between the public- and the private-sector concepts of the public interest will therefore continue unresolved. Ours is
not the period of history that will do otherwise.

MANPOWER PLANNING
IN A PLURALIST ECONOMY

ELI GINZBERG

WE ENCOUNTER SEVERE MISUNDERSTANDINGS when we investigate manpower planning in our pluralist economy. Although we insist on a strict respect for hard social data and although we are anxious about the 8 or 9 million people who have been unemployed in recent years, we continue to rely on terribly poor information and even hazier theorizing.

For a start, it has yet to dawn on us that a quarter of the GNP and at least a third of all jobs are to be found in the not-for-profit activities of government, the educational and medical systems, defense industries, and other institutions. It is no longer realistic to posit a simple dichotomy between public and private sectors of the economy. There are many links between the two, or as I have termed it elsewhere, an inbuilt complementarity.[1]

Our capitalist system relies on nonprofit agencies to train its manpower, to employ those who cannot or do not work for private enterprise, and to sustain the welfare of people living beyond the interplay of market forces. The relationship between public and private institutions is complex and multifaceted. It cannot be gauged alone from the

Eli Ginzberg is the A. Barton Hepburn Professor of Economics and director of the Conservation of Human Resources Project, Columbia University.

[1] "The Pluralistic Economy: A Second Look", in *Scientific American*, December, 1976. I calculated that the not-for-profit sectors accounted in all for 31.9 percent of employment and 26.3 percent of GNP in 1973; these proportions had exactly doubled since 1929.

stark figure that government expenditures account for $700 billion of our
GNP of $1,700 billion.

It might be better to emphasize that public and private institutions
are obliged to plan, separately and together, for a major part of their activities. Of course, the goals and the methods of planning differ strikingly between these sectors, and the differences far exceed the
similarities. The agencies of government perform a set of functions unknown to the private sector. When people look to the federal government to achieve a higher level of employment, to provide health care, or
to stop communism, government cannot plan as if it were charged with
assuring the American consumer of reasonable telephone service.

I do not want to downgrade the problem of providing telephone service, but it is a different assignment than stopping communism. But neither do I want to downgrade the importance of the market. The market
has certain built-in, automatic forces that propel it toward a definable
level of efficiency. Adam Smith would not have included AT&T in his
perception of a market. Perhaps, neither should we. We now appreciate
that those who are regulated have increasingly come to control the
regulators, and this cannot occur in a truly free market.

Regulation makes life complicated for everyone. It takes a lot of time
and resources. Business gets mad at the regulatory bodies. But the industries that are regulated survive; and it is well to remember that business often gets regulated because it asked for it.

So, in a world of oligopoly, not to mention monopoly, we cannot
really have it both ways. We must either rely on markets or we should
admit that we do not. Clearly, there is a real problem when the market
does not work as it should. We must then find some acceptable way of
controlling the use of resources. This is especially true where manpower
is concerned. It is time to recognize that there is not one source of mar-
ketable labor; there are at least six decision-making centers involved.

The first, and the most important, is the individual and the family. It
takes twenty years to prepare a person for work, and much of that preparation goes on within the family. Second, local and state governments
play the major role in providing basic and advanced education; it is an
expensive and a controversial role. Third, nonprofit institutions, such as
private colleges and universities, are crucial producers of trained manpower; they become embroiled, too, in social policy conflict.

Fourth, employers are the major factor in creating jobs and in developing skills. All that happens in terms of preparation is a prelude to what goes on when people start work. Then we encounter a fifth factor: the trade unions and professional societies that are quasi-monopolistic organizations. Their aim is to assure their members who have jobs that they will continue to reap the advantages of their market position. The control and manipulation of job markets is their primary concern.

Finally, the federal government has responsibilities with respect to macroeconomic policy. The amount of this leverage may be much smaller than most people believe. We live in a complicated economy and society, the interrelations among which are not well understood. My new book, *The Human Economy*,[2] tries to set out some of the key relations with which we must deal when we talk about aggregate social policy. Manpower just cannot be viewed as a simple variable or a market instrument.

Recent Manpower Policies

Federal manpower policy comes in many forms and encompasses different modes within the planning process. Up to the great collapse of American capitalism in 1929, we relied on the market and on the individual to take care of almost all manpower problems. There was one major exception. Schooling was a governmental responsibility. Everything else remained the responsibility of the individual, his family, and the employer. There was no way of getting money from the government if one did not work. If a person did not work, he starved, except for handouts from charity. The collapse of the market economy in 1929 was the critical point of change.

The Employment Act of 1946 was the institutional climax of that historic experience. The American people insisted that they were not going to suffer through another era of depression like the 1930s, when millions of hardworking people lost their jobs. The federal government was henceforth committed to doing everything it could to prevent another depression, although nobody knew exactly what it could do.

In a book I recently edited, *Jobs for Americans*,[3] the first essay is by

[2] New York: McGraw-Hill, 1976.   [3] Englewood Cliffs, N.J.: Prentice-Hall, 1976.

Moses Abramovitz. He reviews the experience from 1946 to today and provides a balanced treatment of our successes and failures during this period. He makes it clear that we succeeded not only in avoiding another major depression but also in enlarging the work force from 60 to 90 million workers. We failed in many other regards, but on this critical front we succeeded.

A second point must be made. Our progress on the manpower front was modest and limited. In an initial effort at federal manpower legislation we passed the 1962 Manpower Development and Training Act. Unfortunately, we had misread the evidence. We thought that automation would result in the disemployment of many skilled workers. It turned out, and we knew it within twelve months, that automation had not thrown skilled workers out of work; but the new law helped us recognize a different set of problems. We had a tremendous number of people on the margins who were badly educated and untrained and who encountered grave difficulties in the labor market. In these last decades, the manpower budget moved from an initial annual sum of $52 million to about $4 billion today. There are different ways of counting the total; one way brings the current manpower budget to $9 billion.

As a third point, it should be recalled that in 1963 President Kennedy sent a civil-rights bill up to the Congress without a fair employment section. He was basically interested in desegregating public facilities. Senator Clark asked some of us at that time to testify on discrimination in employment. When this clause was added, Judge Smith (the head of the Rules Committee in the House) thought that he could kill it by adding the word "women." In his view, the Congress would never pass a bill that included women. He was mistaken. As AT&T knows better than most, both sex and race discrimination are now proscribed by the law of the land.

President Johnson inaugurated the War on Poverty by having Congress pass the Economic Opportunity Act in 1964; it included the memorable phrase requiring "maximum feasible participation of the poor." I suspect that the people who slipped in these words had limited perception of what they were doing. The fact that today we have a black man as mayor of Los Angeles, another black man as mayor of Atlanta, and a growing number of blacks in high political office is in part the outcome of these neutral-sounding words. Various poverty programs helped create a training ground for the new black leadership in this country.

Today we have 11 million persons on Aid to Families with Dependent Children (AFDC) at a cost of $9 billion. AFDC is the crux of our welfare system, and it includes 8 million children and 3 million adults. The system blossomed during the 1960s when the country was undergoing its longest period of sustained economic expansion. Nobody planned it that way, and to this day it is not clear just what happened. We might lay the blame on the social workers and the Welfare Mothers' League, or even on partisan politicians. But the truth remains that nobody knows exactly why and how the relief rolls expanded.[4]

In December 1970, President Nixon vetoed the first employment-creation bill that the Congress had passed since the 1930s; six months later he signed a slightly different version. In the interim the political situation had changed. More and more Vietnam veterans needed jobs.

In December 1973 a second job-creation bill was passed, the Comprehensive Employment and Training Act (CETA). When the recession hit in the fall of 1974, Congress added Title VI to expand employment opportunities. It was apparent that we were slowly moving toward federal job creation again.

It would be a mistake to assume, because the federal government has moved back into the business of job creation, that it knows a great deal about how to generate new jobs. It really does not. In the 1970s President Nixon directed the Secretary of Labor to explore how the federal budget could be translated into manpower terms so that we could estimate ahead of time the employment impact of major changes in federal

[4] The aggregate data for 1976 are worth noting. In 1960, the federal welfare budget was $5 billion; in 1976 it was almost $60 billion. In round numbers, it was allocated in the following manner (excepting unemployment insurance):

	dollars, billions	recipients, millions[*]
Medicaid	$15	23
Aid to Families with Dependent Children	9	11
Supplemental Security Income	6	4
Child nutrition	2	25
Food stamps	6	19

* Recipients might obtain more than one form of assistance. There were fewer than the 82 million persons shown receiving family assistance, as the $38 billion total financed many overlapping programs.

expenditures. But the conclusion four years later is that such a methodology is still quite primitive.

What it comes down to is this: the federal government has a limited capacity to affect the employment level except at times when the economy is operating at very low levels. Keynes reached that conclusion in the 1930s. But as my old teacher, J. M. Clark, suggested in his special note to the U.N. committee of experts in 1950, Keynesian economics do not suffice in periods when the economy is closer to full employment and when inflationary pressures are increasing.

In sum, the federal government does much better in spending dollars than in delivering services. What the federal government knows how to do best is to send out Social Security checks on time. That system works very well. But if government has to deliver specific services in every locale, it encounters insuperable difficulties. It was not set up to discharge such responsibilities. The federal government is broadly engaged in only two services, postal and employment office operations. Neither deserves a prize for efficiency.

Another way of putting it is to say that the federal government can have an impact on the society only through changing a group of critical institutions, such as schools, employers, and trade unions; and such changes do not come easily. The information and knowledge bases, as well as the delivery systems, are often grossly inadequate. Much of the time we do not know what we are really trying to affect and change.

In view of these serious omissions, it makes sense to proceed experimentally, one step at a time. Congress and the public are impatient, however; they prefer grandiose programs that promise quick and complete cures. We continue to suffer from excessive expectations. Even when we succeed, we sometimes fail to appreciate our accomplishments because we continue to fall short of idealized expectations.

Most people do not know that the Johnson program to eliminate income poverty in this country has largely succeeded. That does not mean that it is not bad to be poor, or that it is not awful to live in the South Bronx. But we have largely achieved the income goal that was set in the mid 1960s, even allowing for inflation.

This completes my selective review of federal manpower efforts from the vantage of planning. My conclusions? We often set out after the wrong goal; at other times we fail to recognize that we have met the

targets we set for ourselves; at still other times we pursue goals that the
federal government cannot hope to achieve. All told, we have made
progress (to the extent that we have made some) in a most mysterious
fashion.

Manpower and Organization

Every large organization relies heavily on both routine and inertia;
because they slow down change, they allow the organization to continue
working more or less as it did in the past. No large organization can adjust to constant innovation.

Let me illustrate from a case that I know at first hand. In the early
1960s, New York Bell became aware that its labor force and customer
markets were beginning to change radically. The company's officers
asked me to do a study, but when I pressed for top management participation they backed off. They really did not want to look the facts in the
face, and they surely did not want to share their anxieties with an out-
sider.

A new and interesting challenge has emerged within the private
manpower sector: the two-career family. Academics know something
about this and so does the military, and it is going to hit the private sector
very soon. It has important implications for placement, promotion, and
mobility. But I have yet to find a major company that has begun to
tackle the problem.

A second case, which is really related to the first, grows out of the
structure of fringe benefits. They now account for roughly 30 percent of
the wage bill. The old, and still largely ensconced system, provides the
same benefits for everybody. The fact that individuals and families have
different needs, values, and desires is largely ignored. I do not know
how long it will be before large organizations begin to explore the advantages of increasing the options available to their employees. At the
present rate of progress it will be a long time before we accept flexible
packages of retirement and fringe benefits.

The next point is that every large organization must follow the mores
of the society in which it operates. If the society follows discriminatory
practices, the large organization will in most instances follow suit, not

wanting to assume the role of maverick. Small wonder therefore that when a society occasionally changes its values and laws, large organizations become the butt of criticism and legal actions. How could it be otherwise?

Most of the recriminations between business and government leave me unexcited. Business complains about the ineptness of government, about its wastefulness, not to say foolishness. And government sees business as narrowly focused on profit-making, turning its back on the tough social problems and then complaining when government fails to solve them. The National Commission for Manpower Policy, which I chair, has issued a report of its initial discussion with the corporate sector that makes this clear.[5] The large corporations want the government to stay out of their "manpower problems" and focus on doing something for the hard-to-employ. That is fine, but government cannot deal effectively with the seriously disadvantaged all by itself.   2031756

This leads me to a set of observations, albeit conceptual, as fits my role as an economist. First, I have found that the conceptual frameworks with which we work and the concrete realities that confront us do not adequately intersect. The extant body of theory is grossly inadequate. That is why I balk when it is claimed that economic theory can be used to demonstrate that a lower minimum wage would help resolve youth unemployment. I seriously question whether any economic theoretician could prove that on paper, much less in life.

Second, in a world of changing values and power, we discover that all kinds of conflicts are built into our society. There is no escape unless one opts for governance by elites. The conflicts are difficult to resolve and, as a result, the value of any proposed reform (for instance, the Humphrey–Hawkins bill) is hotly contested. If I were a poor black with only intermittent employment, why should I not favor the Humphrey–Hawkins proposal for guaranteed jobs? On the other hand, if I were a corporate executive with an anti-inflation bias, I might be violently opposed to such a radical proposal. It all depends where one is located in the scheme of things.

A third point. It is true that the political process is different from the

<hr/>

[5] *Proceedings of a Conference on the Role of the Business Sector in Manpower Policy,* a special report of the National Commission for Manpower Policy (Washington, D.C.: November 1973).

economic process. But only in part, because the economic process is also heavily political. Every large organization as I understand it is, by definition, a political organization. Its internal divisions can be held together only by the politics of accommodation. That there are differences between the political process in New York City, the federal government, and the workings of AT&T is evident. But there are also many parallels in the ways in which people relate to each other, in how the systems operate, and how they plan, act or react.

Let me, in conclusion, zero in on the overriding manpower issue facing the United States, the question of reducing unemployment. As a people we have belatedly come to recognize that our work ethic has continuing validity only if we offer employable persons an opportunity to work. But as long as we have a serious shortfall in jobs there will be unreconcilable tension between the ethic and the reality. Our social expectations are immense but our capacity and our willingness to translate them into effective action are strictly limited.

Our data tell us that we have 7.5 million persons searching for jobs. My own calculations suggest that the real figure is twice, possibly three times, as large. Millions of people no longer look for jobs because they know that in many places no jobs are available. Clearly, the United States cannot possibly create 5 million new jobs immediately, much less 10 or 15 million. If you ask who are the people who want to work, but who are not now looking, I can identify them as many married women, young people in school, senior citizens, and the seriously handicapped.

To complicate matters further, let me point out that we have developed four separate welfare systems: AFDC, food stamps, supplemental security income, and extended unemployment insurance. There are millions of potential employables, none of whom (except those on unemployment insurance) are counted among the currently unemployed.

At long last we are beginning to face up to the dilemma. A society that says it believes in the work ethic must be concerned with assuring employable persons the opportunity to work. This social priority is reflected in the Humphrey–Hawkins bill and in the speeches of the chairman of the Federal Reserve Board; Arthur Burns has expressed his belief that the government should act as the employer of last resort. Burns talked of government jobs at 10 percent below the minimum wage. Marcia Freedman of my staff has recently written a book on *Labor Markets:*

Segments and Shelters.[6] She points out that two out of every five jobs fail to pay enough to enable a wage earner to support a family. Hence our concern must be with both jobs and income—not only with jobs but also with good jobs. Here is a challenge that will keep us busy for quite some time to come!

[6] Montclair, N.J.: Allan Held, Osmun, 1976.

Discussion

The Reserve Army of the Unemployed

ROBERT LEKACHMAN. I would like to explore a different set of interpretations than Eli Ginzberg. I agree with him that in the thirty years since the Employment Act of 1946 we have, indeed, succeeded in avoiding a major depression. But I cannot agree that we have treated the problems of unemployment with the urgency they deserve.

We need not enter into conspiracy theories to suggest that unemployment serves a useful economic function. Not as a result of the malice of any particular group, our society has come to appreciate the contingency roles played by "the reserve army of the unemployed." Depending on the circumstances, they help discourage labor militancy, union bargaining, absenteeism, or the pressure to raise wages.

In a business-minded society, corporate interests find an 8 percent unemployment rate far more tolerable than do their employees. In recent years we have seen both profits and unemployment rising. I attribute our slow, faltering attempts to deal with unemployment to the inability of our coalition style of politics to create jobs. The proposals put forward in the Humphrey–Hawkins bill were never impressive. What was impressive, however, was the determination of business interests to block the bill's congressional passage. That they prevailed, even in an election year when Congress was dominated by the Democrats, is truly significant. Congress chose to live with continuing unemployment rather than dare to legislate structural changes in the U.S. economy.

MURRAY WEIDENBAUM. The trouble with this analysis is that it overlooks the serious repercussions of contemporary inflation. The government deficits that prompted the inflationary upsurge, and the massive welfare spending that served as a depressant to manpower policy, just cannot be overlooked. Inflation and economic recession are more forceful than any presumption of political pressures in maintaining unemployment.

DAVID APTER. The factor of inflation is critically important for reasons that extend beyond those just cited. When the middle class finds its savings, its pension equity, its educational privileges, and its income threatened, it begins to act for the first time as a class. It shows more anxiety about the printing of money than about the fate of the idle poor. It moves away from a sense of civility or civic responsibility to take care of its own material interests. It looses its sense of guilt about the welfare muddle and the squalor of poverty. It becomes anxious about stabilizing social conflicts, and it refuses to pay the substantial guilt money that would be needed to finance extensive reforms.

ELI GINZBERG. It would be helpful if we really knew what could or should be done to remove unemployment. The most feasible area for political action today appears in the linkage of work and welfare. Both conservatives and liberals are interested in providing work for people who receive income transfer payments. Aside from using macropolicy to stimulate the entire economy, I think we will have to pay greater attention to the intolerable defects of the social welfare system.

In the near future we must expand job opportunities for youth through public service jobs and through government support for the employment, in the private and nonprofit sectors, of employable people who now subsist on welfare. A target to create 2.5 million new jobs a year, as President Ford recommended, appears sensible and realistic. Anything less would impose social hardship and perpetuate an intolerable wastage of human resources.

Public Policy and Unemployment

ELI GINZBERG. The critical question concerns the cause of all of this social hardship and job failure. Is it a malfunctioning of the market? Is it a desire to have the market function so that a considerable amount of unemployment is always present? Does it have to do with the unusual demographic trends that led to such a large inflow of young people? Does it reflect the structural transformations resulting from the large numbers of women entering the labor market?

It has to do with all of these developments.

To assume that unemployment is a single or simplistic phenomenon, the end result of only one cause, is ridiculous. And that is why any simplistic cure is ridiculous. One must sort out the complex factors at work. For example, most people who are unemployed are not in poverty. That is extremely important. Poverty and unemployment overlap only at the margin. A significant proportion of all people who are unemployed at any one time are voluntarily unemployed. They are moving from New York to Los Angeles, they are leaving a job to return to school or to have a baby. We simply must sort out these multiple reasons why people are unemployed if we are to design responsive policies.[7]

Moreover, we have developed elaborate support systems that influence employment outcomes. The provision of extensive benefits has often encouraged people to remain unemployed. It is also likely that many of the women on AFDC in New York City work on the side and do not report their earnings; otherwise they would have no discretionary income. There are many kinds of money transfers and many kinds of work problems. We are concerned about people who want to work, who want to be related to the society through work, and who lack the opportunity to work or to earn an adequate income.

I would place a high priority on finding work for youngsters in the ghetto, and it must be work with a future. There is too much opportunity for youngsters to earn income from criminal or illicit activities. Either one links people to society through work or they have no stake in its preservation. I lived in Germany before Hitler, and it is clear to me that Hitler's coming into office had more to do with large-scale unemployment than with Germany's defeat in World War I.

Let me emphasize that I do not want to persuade everybody to work, nor can any democratic society require everyone to work. But what we should do is to provide an opportunity for work for the young, the disadvantaged, for women, and for anyone who recognizes that work is a vital element in individual and social life. We should not repeat the error that Adam Smith made. He said that the only kind of productive work was

[7] Dean Morse pointed out in *The Peripheral Worker* (New York: Columbia University Press, 1969), that almost 45 percent of the persons who are employed work less than full time or for a full year. The data suggest that 30 percent of the work performed is handled by less-than-full-time workers.

work that resulted in physical output. There are many meaningful types of work, such as helping the aged or voluntary work, that are not directly goods-producing. Many citizens and society as a whole would profit from these types of work, so we should ensure that such job opportunities are potentially available.

As far as job motivation and satisfaction are concerned, it must be admitted that only a small proportion of all persons who have jobs really work hard. Though gainfully employed, few workers find dignity or adequate satisfaction in their work. I do not want to be self-righteous about the poor, about their motives or their productivity. If we do not make room for everybody who wants to work, we will buy trouble. Given our economic system, there will always be some unemployment, but we need not stand idly by while millions of people seek jobs that hold some promise of a future. What we must do is to relax our rigid attitudes toward the funding of welfare, the provision of more work opportunities, and toward the idle—whether they are rich or poor.

In Eastern Europe, everyone has a job because the Communist regimes reject the idea of handing out welfare. People must work for their income. I can still see the seventy-year-old women in Sofia, in mid-January, breaking up ice with ancient implements. Is this compulsory work better than welfare? Is it better for the government to force people to take work "of last resort"? Or should we mail out more relief checks so that people can perform some useful social service and enjoy their leisure?

The Israelis also believe that everybody should work, though in the process they pay relatively little attention to productivity. There are trade-offs, and in my view the Israelis are right; given their immigrant problems, everybody has to be linked into the work system, even if the work they do is often low in its value-added character.

Denying people a chance to participate in their society is dangerous, especially if young people are kept idle. If we were smarter, we could moderate the unemployment problem by dividing it up differently. Instead of 8 million unemployed, many of whom have been out of work for long periods, suppose we were able to ask 80 million Americans to work 10 percent less? It would make quite a difference. Some of the European governments, the UAW, and even AT&T have begun to experiment along these lines, and we should pay attention to their findings.

The Economies of Manpower Utilization

MURRAY WEIDENBAUM. I must return to the issues of inflation and the consequent decline of living standards. In the past our generosity in extending welfare, family, and unemployment benefits was financed by the vigorous growth and expansion of the economy. More was produced and therefore more could be shared. Living standards rose, and it was less burdensome to pay for people who did not work.

These trends have now been reversed. We argue strongly over which policy priorities should be pursued. Should we first aim to curb the erosive effects of inflation; or should we immediately provide millions of marginal jobs in a society that has bolstered itself against the worst consequences of unemployment? For all of our talk about the Protestant work ethic, we cannot ignore the decreasing productivity that will materialize if we pay too many people for too little work with highly devalued dollars.

WALTER GOLDSTEIN. I would like to raise the issue on the obverse side of macroeconomic policy. We might not know how best to utilize manpower resources but there is a suspicious delay in trying to find solutions. The conservative bias in business and on campus is more pervasive than we admit. We prefer, it seems, to perpetuate social hardship and injustice rather than to reconstruct our economic system or to redistribute the benefits of economic growth.

In the northeastern United States we have seen a considerable decline in industry. Over 600,000 manufacturing jobs in New York City were eliminated in the last seven years. The flight of industry has left the people of New York with only the gloomiest prospects for economic regeneration. Since it is difficult for the least employable citizens to move, either to the Sunbelt or to carefully zoned suburbs, what should be done for these millions of immobile and marginal citizens? Simply counsel them to resign their lives to futility while we reformulate our economic models and recycle our political axioms? There is a callous tone to the conventional wisdom that urges the cause of inaction. It moves us, on good business principles, to leave festering ghettos alone simply because we do not know how to provide work for the unfortunate wretches who are condemned to live in them.

There is a hypothesis that for every 1 percent reduction in the rate of unemployment there can be a 3.4 percent increment in GNP and a $15 billion rise in government revenues. If this is correct, there would be handsome returns accruing to the economy from investments in public housing, city services, and job expansion. At the present time, our political platitudes declare that we cannot "throw money at social problems"—to arrest the pauperizing of the cities, of their school systems, and of their welfare facilities. What we need is a political stimulus to channel investment into the non-profit work, the service sector, and the welfare-oriented jobs that run-down cities can offer. If meaningful work is to be found for the undertrained and the underprivileged, it seems that the poor will have to provide the political stimulus, themselves. I dread to think how society will respond, however, if they ever resolve to take realistic or aggressive action toward this end.

We live in a work economy, as well as in a money economy, as the 45 percent of black youth unemployed in the inner-city ghettos will tell you. They, too, want to work and share in what others enjoy, including rewarding jobs and promising career opportunities.

ELI GINZBERG. I must answer again that there are no simple solutions. We can establish policy priorities, such as enlarging the defense industries (if we worry about a Soviet threat); or enabling all qualified applicants to go to college; or enlarging the advertising industry in order to boost consumer spending. However ill-advised, these efforts would help create jobs, train manpower, and enlarge the GNP. But they might not be the wisest policies to choose. Perhaps there are better ways of spending the surplus that our society creates.

I do not believe that all the problems we face reflect a shortage of dollars. Often the difficulty lies with using the dollars better. For instance, the federal government spends about $2 billion annually on youth programs and the return is very low. Or take the fact that New York City spends about $8 billion annually on human resource services, for education, health, welfare, and child support. This sum has risen from under $2 billion in the 1960s, but there has been no change in

the city's population and the quality of its services has not been significantly improved with many more dollars. Money plagues the Defense
Department, too. It now finds that manpower overhead support is so expensive that it can put very few troops into the front lines for a budget of
$80 billion (excluding hardware procurement).

Regrettably, we do not have the control structures or the institutional
mechanisms to know where many of these program funds end up. Of the
billions allocated for Medicare, or for New York City's social services,
vast amounts flow to the middle-class professionals in charge, many of
whom just push paper around.

Nor is it a useful answer to recommend that we move from service
sector transfers to market allocations. We cannot put the Pentagon, the
New York subways, GM, or AT&T back into the free market. Initiative in the automobile industry was not restricted to Henry Ford; it was
also shared by the lobbyists for the Highway Trust. They knew that in a
pluralistic economy the government had to build the highways if the industry was to expand its product base. Trying to build a new market, by
giving funds to Medicaid consumers, proved to be erroneous. The system exploited the customers, and the illusion of creating a new market
cost us a misplaced fortune.

In my essay on the complementarity of the public and private sectors
of the U.S. economy,[8] I arrived at five conclusions. Let me finish this
presentation by summarizing them:

1. The U.S. economy is still dependent on a large and healthy private
   sector, but it locates 1 out of 3 jobs in not-for-profit activities.
2. The service rather than the goods-producing industries account for
   an ever greater part of employment; less than one-third of our
   manpower is occupied in manufacturing activity.
3. The measurement of productivity is so rough (particularly with respect to services) that concerns about the retardation in the growth
   of productivity may be exaggerated.
4. The division of the adult population into workers and nonworkers
   is no longer realistic.
5. An advanced service economy trains its manpower in the not-for-
   profit sector. On that basis alone, the complementarity of the public and private sectors must be fully acknowledged.

[8] "The Pluralistic Economy: A Second Look."

THE SECOND
MANAGERIAL REVOLUTION

*The Shift of Economic Decision – Making
from Business to Government*

MURRAY L. WEIDENBAUM

THE CHANGE NOW TAKING PLACE in business–government relations in
the United States is so pervasive that it represents a "second managerial
revolution." The current wave of government planning and regulation of
business is changing the locus of decision-making and of responsibility
for a large portion of private sector activities.

The first managerial revolution was noted by Berle and Means more
than four decades ago and given a name by James Burnham three decades ago. They were referring to the shift of decision-making power
from the formal owners of the modern corporation to professional managers. Currently business decision-making is shifting from the professional management selected by the corporation itself to the vast corps of

Murray L. Weidenbaum is director of the Center for the Study of American Business at
Washington University, in Saint Louis.

government planners and regulators who are influencing and often controlling the key managerial decisions of the typical business firm.

This second managerial revolution is forcing a fundamental change in the nature of our society. The traditional concerns and debates in business–government relations ("Are we moving toward socialism?" "Are we in the grip of a military–industrial complex?") should be recognized as dealing with an age that already has passed. There are few important examples of outright nationalization of industry in the United States. Rather, the tendency is for government to take over or at least share many of the key aspects of decision-making of all firms.[1]

The change that our industrial economy is undergoing must be understood as a bureaucratic phenomenon. In the main, it is not intentional, or even noticeable to the day-to-day observer. What is involved are the lawful efforts of governmental civil servants going about their routine and assigned activities, tasks which in concept are hard to speak ill of. Who is opposed to cleaning up the environment? Or enhancing job safety? Or improving consumer products? Or eliminating discrimination? Or promoting full employment?

The Changing Locus of Economic Decision-making

Extending the analysis of Berle, Means, and Burnham to the current situation, it is not who owns the means of production but who makes the key decisions that is crucial in determining the relative distribution of public and private power. If we step back and assess the long-term impacts on the private enterprise system that flow from the rapidly growing host of government inspections, regulations, reviews, and subsidies, we find that the entire business–government relationship is being changed in the process. To be sure, the process is far from complete, and it proceeds unevenly in its various phases. But the results are clear enough: the government increasingly is participating in and often con-

---

[1] For details, see Murray L. Weidenbaum, *Government-Mandated Price Increases* (Washington, D.C.: American Enterprise Institute for Public Policy Research, 1975); Murray L. Weidenbaum, *Business, Government, and the Public* (Englewood Cliffs, N.J.: Prentice-Hall, 1977).

trolling the kinds of decisions which are at the heart of the capitalistic system.

It is important to understand that this relatively silent bureaucratic revolution is not intended to undermine the capitalistic system. The men and women involved are patriotic citizens who are attempting to carry out high-priority national objectives that are considered to be basic to the quality of life in America.

Yet those who have assigned them these tasks, the Congress and the executive-branch leadership, often have failed to appreciate the significance of what they are doing. If specific laws had been proposed or regulations promulgated for the government formally to take over private risk-bearing and initiative, the problem would have been faced head on, and the changes probably defeated. It is significant that the most ambitious proposals to extend government influence over the private sector, such as the full employment and balanced growth act of 1976 (the Humphrey–Hawkins bill), refer to encouraging the "optimum contribution of the private sector" and to the desire to "foster and promote free competitive enterprise." That of course is one of the most significant and difficult aspects of the development that we are analyzing. This silent managerial revolution is unintentional. It is merely an unexpected by-product—but far more than a minor side effect—of the expanding role of government in our modern society. Most of the proponents of greater government planning and regulation truly believe that this ambitious activity can be superimposed on the business system without damaging its central and desirable features, such as risk-taking, efficiency and productivity, scientific progress, and enhanced employment opportunities.

The expansion of government involvement is self-reinforcing. When the government issues rules and regulations that reduce the ability of the private sector to provide productive employment, the pressures rise for government to serve as the employer of last resort. When government policies add to the cost of private production, that can be a strong justification for greater governmental involvement in wage and price decisions. And when government policies sharply curtail the ability of the private sector to generate adequate savings to finance economic growth, not only is the government looked upon as the banker of last resort, but the basic vitality of the capitalistic system is called into question.

The New Wave of Government Regulation

It is hard to overestimate the rapid expansion of government involvement in business in the United States which is now occurring. The new type (and the almost infinite variety) of governmental regulation of business is not limited to the traditional regulatory agencies, such as the Interstate Commerce Commission, the Civil Aeronautics Board, the Federal Communications Commission, and the Federal Power Commission. Rather, the line operating departments and bureaus of government—the Departments of Agriculture, Commerce, Health-Education-Welfare, Interior, Justice, Labor, Transportation, and the Treasury—are now involved in actions that affect virtually every firm.

Certainly most public policy changes affecting business–government relations in recent years have been in the direction of greater governmental involvement: environmental controls, job safety inspections, equal employment opportunity enforcement, consumer product safety regulations, energy restrictions, and recording and reporting of items varying from domestic illnesses to foreign currency transactions. Indeed, when we attempt to look at the emerging business–government relationship from the business executive's viewpoint, a very considerable public presence is evident in what ostensibly, or at least historically, have been private affairs.

No business official today, neither the head of a large company nor the corner grocer, can operate without considering a multitude of governmental restrictions and regulations. Costs and profits can be affected as much by a bill passed in Washington as by a management decision in the front office or a customer's decision at the checkout counter. The types of management decisions which increasingly are subject to governmental influence, review, or control are fundamental to the business system: what lines of business to go into, what products can be produced, which investments can be financed, under what conditions can products be produced, where can they be made, how can they be marketed, what prices can be charged, what profit can be made?

Virtually every major department of the typical industrial corporation in the United States has one or more counterparts in a federal agency that controls or strongly influences its internal decision-making. The scientists in corporate research laboratories now receive much of their

guidance from lawyers in federal, state, and local regulatory agencies.
The engineers in manufacturing departments must abide by standards
promulgated by Labor Department authorities. The sales personnel in
marketing organizations must follow procedures established by government administrators in safety agencies. The location of facilities must be
in conformance with a variety of environmental statutes. The activities of
personnel staffs are increasingly restricted by the various executive
agencies concerned with employment conditions, and are subject to
court review. Finance departments often bear the brunt of the rising
paperwork burden being imposed on business by government agencies
which seem to assume that information is a free good—or in any event
that more is always better than less.

When we examine the sector of industry that already is most subject
to government supervision, defense production, the results are disconcerting. It is precisely the companies that are most heavily dependent
on military contracts that report the largest cost overruns and the greatest delays. The society does not get the benefit of efficiency and innovation expected from private industry. The ultimate consequences of
governmental assumption of basic entrepreneurial and managerial functions is surely a topic worthy of considerable attention and study.

This is a phenomenon still in the process of development, rather than
one that has attained a "steady state." The basic factors causing the
change are diverse, ranging from the concern by some with the quality
of life to the desire by others to increase the social responsiveness of
business enterprise. Yet, proposals for changes in public policy affecting
business are virtually all variations on a single predictable theme: to
increase the scope and degree of governmental involvement while shifting costs from the federal treasury to the products and services that
consumers buy.

It is not just a matter of "more of the same." The current wave of government regulation is not merely an intensification of traditional activities; in good measure, it is a new departure. The standard theory of
government regulation of business, which is still in general use and has
dominated professional and public thinking on the subject, is based on
the model of the Interstate Commerce Commission. Under this approach, a federal commission is established to regulate a specific industry, with the related concern of promoting the well-being of that

industry. Often the public or consumer interest is subordinated, or even ignored, as the agency focuses on the needs and concerns of the industry that it is regulating.

In some cases, because of the unique expertise possessed by members of the industry or because of its job enticements for regulators who leave government employment, the regulatory commission may become a captive of the industry it is supposed to regulate. At least, this is a popularly held view of the development of the regulatory process. Actual practice of course varies by agency and jurisdiction and over time. In addition to the ICC, other examples of this development which have been cited from time to time include the Civil Aeronautics Board, the Federal Communications Commission, the Federal Power Commission, and the Federal Maritime Commission.

Although the traditional type of federal regulation of business surely continues, Congress's recent efforts at regulation follow, in the main, a fundamentally different pattern. Evaluating the activities of these newer regulatory efforts with the ICC model is inappropriate and can lead to undesirable public policy. The new federal regulatory agencies are simultaneously broader in the scope of their jurisdiction than the ICC-CAB-FCC-FPC model, yet in important aspects they are far more restricted. This anomaly lies at the heart of the problem of relating their efforts to the national interest.

In the cases of the Environmental Protection Agency (EPA), the Equal Employment Opportunity Commission (EEOC), the Consumer Product Safety Commission, the Occupational Safety and Health Administration (OSHA), and the new Energy Department, the regulatory agency is not limited to a single industry. Each of these relative newcomers to the federal bureaucracy has a jurisdiction that extends to the bulk of the private sector and at times to productive activities in the public sector itself. It is this far-ranging characteristic that makes it impractical for any single industry to dominate these regulatory activities in the manner of the traditional model. What specific industry is going to capture the EEOC or OSHA, or would have the incentive to do so?

In comparison to the older agencies oriented to specific industries, the newer federal regulators operate in a very different way. They are not concerned with the totality of a company or industry, but only with the narrow segment of operations falling under their jurisdiction. The

ICC, for example, must pay attention to the basic mission of the trucking industry, to provide transportation services to the public, as part of its supervision of rates and entry into the trucking business. The EPA, on the other hand, is interested almost exclusively in the effect of trucking operations on the environment. This limitation prevents the agency from developing a close concern with the overall well-being of any one company or industry. Instead, it can result in a total lack of concern over the effects of its specific actions on a company or industry.

If any special interest may come to dominate such a functionally oriented agency, it is the group preoccupied with its specific task— ecologists, unions, civil rights groups, or consumerists. Thus, little if any attention may be given to the basic mission of the industry to provide goods and services to the public. Also ignored are crosscutting concerns or matters broader than the specific charter of the regulating agency, such as productivity, economic growth, employment, cost to the consumer, effects on overall living standards, and inflationary impacts. While the traditional regulatory agencies may be said to be overly concerned at times with economic growth and productive efficiency, the newer programs are moved by different interests. Their impetus comes from such social considerations as improving the quality of life, both on and off the job, and changing the distribution of income so as to achieve greater equity among the various groups in society.

To be sure, there are important cases which blend the old and new forms of regulation. The Securities and Exchange Commission is a good example. In one aspect of its activities, it regulates a specific branch of the economy, the securities industry. Yet many of its rules also influence the way in which a great many companies prepare their financial statements and reports to shareholders. Economy-wide regulatory agencies are not a recent creation. The Federal Trade Commission has existed for years. Moreover, a few one-industry agencies continue to be created, notably the Commodity Futures Trading Commission. This new commission regulates the financial markets dealing with products of agriculture and other extractive industries.

The result of the new approach to government regulation of business is the reverse of the traditional situation. Rather than being dominated by a given industry, the newer type of federal regulatory activity is far more likely to utilize the resources of various industries, or to ignore their needs, in order to further the specific objectives of the agency. Strange and varying alliances arise in promoting a given type of regulatory activity, or in pushing for reform. The business firms and labor unions in a given regulated industry often become strong supporters of the traditional industry-oriented commission which they have learned to live with, if not to dominate. They may join ranks to oppose efforts by consumer groups and economists to cut back on the extent of the "protective" regulation.

In contrast, consumer groups advocate expanding the newer types of crosscutting or functional regulation. They often are joined by labor groups, particularly in the occupational health area. Here, reform efforts may be led by coalitions of business groups and economists, who are concerned with the excessive costs and other consequences of the specialized regulatory activities. These alliances may shift from time to time. Specific safety regulations for automobiles may be opposed by both unions and companies in the motor vehicle industry—although the two groups may differ strongly on job safety standards. The older consumer organizations may become more concerned with the ultimate cost to the consumer of expanding governmental activities than are the newer and more militant groups that emphasize public control over private sector activities.

The Costs of Government Involvement in Business Decision-making

Even though most of the changes in governmental control of business decision-making are designed to benefit the public, one neglected aspect is increasingly apparent as the widening arrays of regulations take their full effect: the consumer ultimately pays the added costs that so often result. This is especially true in the case of the newer regulatory programs which are the special concern of this study—the functional or cross-industry types of social legislation. In the more traditional areas, many regulations deal with natural monopolies such as utilities. In some of these one-industry regulatory efforts, however, the government's actions may be anticompetitive and thus ultimately costly to the consumer. Interstate trucking furnishes a cogent example, where federal regulation is in large degree a barrier to entry, protecting existing firms against possible new entrants.

There are many ways in which government regulation can increase the cost of production and thus the prices that consumers pay. Productivity in particular is often adversely affected by the various regulations designed to improve the quality of the work environment. To the extent that the regulations reduce accidents and absenteeism, they do indeed contribute positively to output and thus to economic welfare. But in practice the emphasis is on essentially "bureaucratic" concerns. Forms are filled out. Safety rules are posted. Inspections take place. Fines are levied. But no significant reduction in industrial accident rates has resulted.

In the case of the job safety program, as in numerous other areas of government involvement, the original concern of the public and the Congress has been converted to the practice of not violating the rules and regulations. "You won't get into trouble if you don't violate the safety standards," is the response, even if as many accidents occur as before. The emphasis shifts to such trivia as raising and answering these types of questions: How big is a hole? When is a roof a floor? How frequently must spittoons be cleaned? The results in terms of the safety objective are almost invariably disappointing. Yet the reaction is virtually predictable: redouble the existing effort—more forms, more inspections, and thus higher costs to the taxpayer and higher prices to the consumer.

Examples of obvious inefficiencies or trivia in regulation of business are not hard to come by. Capable, intelligent, and well-meaning administrators delegating decisions to capable, intelligent, and well-meaning subordinates cannot specify in advance all of the correct or desirable exceptions to general rules. Upon examination, the reported examples of regulatory nonsense often do not turn out to be mere flukes. They are almost an inevitable result of the rapid expansion of the scope and variety of regulatory functions that has occurred in the United States in recent years.

Federal regulation has other costs to the economy. It also affects the prospects for economic growth and productivity by levying a claim for an increasing share of new capital formation. This is most evident in the environmental and safety areas, and its importance can be observed quite readily.

An examination of the flow of capital spending by American manufacturing companies just before the recent recession is revealing. In 1969, the total new investment in plant and equipment in the entire manufacturing sector came to $26 billion. The annual totals rose in the following years. When the effect of inflation is eliminated, however, it can be seen that four years later, in 1973, total capital spending by U.S. manufacturing companies was no higher. In "real terms," it was approximately $26 billion in both years.

That is not the end of the story, however. In 1973, a much larger proportion of capital outlays was devoted to meeting government regulatory requirements in the pollution and safety area—$3 billion more, to be specific. Hence, although the economy and its needs had been growing substantially in those four years, the real annual investment in modernization and new capital had actually been declining. The situation was worsened by the accelerated rate at which existing manufacturing facilities were being closed down because the rapidly rising costs of meeting government regulations meant that they were no longer economically viable. About 350 foundries in the United States were closed during 1971–1974 because they could not meet requirements such as those imposed by the Environmental Protection Agency and the Occupational Safety and Health Administration. This may help to explain why the American economy, for a substantial part of 1973, appeared to lack needed productive capacity, despite what had been large nominal investments in new plant and equipment in recent years.

The governmental decision-making process can have other adverse effects on capital formation by introducing uncertainty about the future of regulations governing the introduction of new processes and products. An example is furnished in a November 1975 report of a task force of the President's Energy Resources Council dealing with the possibility of developing a new synthetic fuel industry. In evaluating the impact of the Federal Water Pollution Control Act Amendments of 1972, the task force reported, "It would be next to impossible at this time to predict the impact of these requirements on synthetic fuels production."[2]

With reference to the National Environmental Policy Act of 1969, the task force stated that the major uncertainty was not whether a project would be allowed to proceed, but rather the length of time that it would

[2] Synfuels Interagency Task Force, *Recommendations for a Synthetic Fuels Commericalization Program*, report submitted to the President's Energy Resources Council, vol. 1 (Washington, D.C.: Government Printing Office, 1975), p. C-22.

be delayed pending the issuance of an environmental impact statement that would stand up in court. The task force pointed out that "the cost of such delays (construction financing and inflated raw materials and labor costs) is an obvious potential hazard to any synfuels project." In evaluating the overall impact of government regulatory activity, the task force concluded that "some of these requirements could easily hold up or permanently postpone any attempt to build and operate a synthetic fuels plant."[3]

Government regulation, albeit unintentionally, can have strongly adverse effects on employment. This has been demonstrated in the minimum-wage area, where teenagers have increasingly been priced out of labor markets. One recent study has shown that as a result of the 1966 increase in the statutory minimum wage, teenage employment in the United States in 1972 was 320,000 lower than it otherwise would have been. That one increase in the compulsory minimum wage meant that the youth unemployment rate in 1972 was 3.8 percentage points higher than otherwise would have been the case.[4]

In the construction labor area, where unemployment rates are substantially above the national average, government regulation also acts to price some segment of the work force out of competitive labor markets. Under the Davis-Bacon legislation, the Secretary of Labor promulgates "prevailing" wages to be paid on federal and federally supported construction projects. A number of studies have shown that these federally mandated wage rates are often above those prevailing in the labor market where the work is to be done.[5]

Perhaps to a minor degree the equal employment opportunity program may increase unemployment by delaying the filling of job vacancies. To the extent that employers must undertake protracted job searches before hiring employees, the average time of unemployment is likely to be longer. It is not uncommon for a position to remain unfilled despite the presence of an adequate labor supply at market prices, be-

[3] Ibid., pp. C-18, C-134.
[4] James F. Ragan, Jr., *Minimum Wage Legislation and the Youth Labor Market,* Working Paper no. 8, Center for the Study of American Business, Washington University (St. Louis, 1976), p. 29.
[5] John P. Gould, *Davis-Bacon Act* (Washington, D.C.: American Enterprise Institute for Public Policy Research, 1971); Armand J. Thieblot, Jr., *The Davis-Bacon Act* (Philadelphia: University of Pennsylvania, Wharton School, 1975).

cause the governmental regulatory requirements have not been met.

The key price that the nation may be paying for the expansion of governmental power is the attenuation of the risk-bearing and entrepreneurial characteristics of the private enterprise system which, at least in the past, have contributed so effectively to rapid rates of innovation, productivity, growth, and progress. One hidden cost of federal regulation is the reduced rate of innovation that occurs as the result of governmental restrictions. The longer that it takes for some change to be approved by a federal regulatory agency (a new or improved product, a more efficient production process), the less likely that the change will be made.

As William D. Carey of the American Association for the Advancement of Science has stated, "Government may imagine that it is neutral toward the rate and quality of technological risk-taking, but it is not. . . . Regulatory policies aimed at the public interest rarely consider impacts on innovation."[6] The adverse effect of regulation on innovation is likely to be felt more strongly by smaller firms and thus have an anticompetitive impact. According to Dr. Mitchell Zavon, president of the American Association of Poison Control Centers,

We've got to the point in regulatory action where it's become so costly and risky to bring out products that only the very largest firms can afford to engage in these risky ventures. To bring out a new pesticide you have to figure a cost of $7,000,000 and seven years of time.[7]

To the degree that management attention is diverted from traditional product development, production, and marketing concerns to meeting governmentally imposed social requirements, a significant but subtle bureaucratization of corporate activity may result. In the employee pension area, for example, the recently enacted employee-pension regulation has shifted much of the concern of pension-fund managers from maximizing the return on the contributions to following a more cautious approach of minimizing the likelihood that the fund managers will be criticized for their investment decisions. It thus becomes safer—although not necessarily more desirable to the employees covered—for

[6] William D. Carey, "Muddling Through: Government and Technology," *Science*, 4 April 1975, p. 13.

[7] Quoted by Sheila Rule, "Pesticide Regulations Called Too Stringent," *St. Louis Post-Dispatch*, 18 September 1974, p. 18F.

the pension managers to keep more detailed records of their delibera-
tions, to hire more outside experts (so that the responsibility can be
diluted), and to avoid innovative investments.

The foolishness and uneconomical effects that can flow from government regulation pale when they are compared to the arbitrary power
that can be exerted by the personnel of the regulatory agencies. Many
liberals are outraged by the arbitrary "no-knock" powers of federal investigative agencies, yet they readily ignore the unchallenged no-knock
power used by federal agencies in their regulation of private business.

The Supreme Court has ruled that air pollution inspectors do not
need search warrants to enter the property of suspected polluters as
long as they do not enter areas closed to the public. The unannounced
inspections, which were conducted without warrants, were held to be
not in violation of constitutional protections against unreasonable search
and seizure. The inspectors of the Labor Department's Occupational
Safety and Health Administration (OSHA) can go farther. They have no-
knock power to enter the premises of virtually any business in the
United States, without a warrant or even prior announcement, to in-
spect for health and safety violations. Jail terms are provided in the
OSHA law for anyone tipping off a "raid."

The awesome power exercised by government regulators often goes
unappreciated by the public as well as by the regulators themselves.
The case of the ban on spray adhesives is worthy of some attention. On
the surface, it appears to have been at most only a matter of excessive
caution on the part of the Consumer Product Safety Commission.

On August 20, 1973, the commission banned certain brands of aerosol
spray adhesives as an imminent hazard. Its decision was based primarily
on the preliminary findings of one academic researcher who claimed that
they could cause birth defects. After more careful research failed to cor-
roborate the initial report, the commission lifted the ban on March 1,
1974. Why do I mention this case? Depriving consumers of spray adhesives for less than 7 months does not seem to be too harsh in view of the
desire to avoid serious threats to people's health. In fact, the admission
of error on the part of the commission is commendable. Its prompt re-
scission of the initial action would almost seem to break speed records
for a government agency.

But there is more to the story. It seems that a number of pregnant

women who had used the spray adhesives reacted to the news of the
commission's initial decision by undergoing abortions for fear of producing babies with birth defects. They could not reverse their decisions
when the regulatory commission reversed its. The sadness of this case is
hardly reduced by the fact that everyone involved was trying to promote
the public health and safety. Indeed, this case illustrates the dilemma of
government regulators. Had the commission failed to ban spray adhesives and the initial research subsequently been validated, an equally
sad scenario could have resulted.[8]

Feedback Effects on Business Decision-making

The power of government regulators also can give rise to a feedback
effect on private decision-making, and some of those feedbacks can be
extremely negative from both public and private viewpoints. The highly
publicized, illegal gifts by business corporations may have been in part a
response to this phenomenon. Frankly, that assertion will need a bit of
explaining to avoid future misunderstanding.

Business has been taking it on the chin as revelations of so-called political slush funds have been uncovered. It is altogether fitting that
lawbreaking be exposed and punished. Corporate contributions to federal election campaigns are illegal. Yet these illegal business contributions to political causes have another aspect that has been ignored.
When we look at more traditional types of crime, we find that progressive thinking is not limited to punishment. By identifying the conditions
that breed crime, we hope that public policy can be modified so as to
reduce or eliminate those conditions—a preventive approach to lawbreaking.

A parallel can be drawn to the Watergate-related cases of unlawful
corporate political contributions and their attempted cover-up. What
was the underlying motive for these illegal acts? The dominant motive
was not usually a desire to enrich the individual executives who were in-

[8] Comptroller General of the United States, *Banning of Two Toys and Certain Aerosol
Spray Adhesives,* MWD-75-65 (Washington, D.C.: U.S. General Accounting Office, 1975),
pp. 13–30; Jerry E. Bishop, "Move to Halt Selling of Spray Adhesives Prompted Abortions," *Wall Street Journal,* 10 February 1976, p. 11.

volved, or even to enhance their positions in their companies. Neither was the typical motive the desire to get the federal government to grant a particular favor to the firm ("favors" in the form of government contracts were the object of many of the companies' payments to citizens of other nations).

Rather, the illegal campaign contributions were usually a response, often reluctant, to requests from political representatives of a powerful governmental administration that could do great harm to the company. The possibility that the government would abuse its vast power in the absence of an adequate payment was a risk that many corporate managements decided not to take.

Not surprisingly, many of the executives who were implicated held positions in corporations that are dependent on the government in important ways—for defense contracts in the case of large manufacturing companies, for government-approved route structures in the case of airlines, and for special subsidies in the case of natural resource industries. It may not be too wide of the mark to consider many of those illegal corporate payments as a form of "protection" money given to prevent action harmful to the company. Viewed in this light, the underlying cause of this particular type of white-collar crime does not arise within the company itself. Rather, the fundamental reason for the lawbreaking is the tremendous and arbitrary power that the society has given the federal government over the private sector.

Thus the eradication of this form of white-collar crime involves more than tighter auditing standards and improved laws on political financing, although such changes are surely necessary. It also requires restraint in further expansion of governmental power over the private sector. From this point of view, it would be helpful to reduce the arbitrary decision-making authority that many federal agencies now possess in their dealings with business firms.

My basic point should not be misunderstood. Lawbreaking, whether by business executives or others, should not be condoned. It should be ferreted out and punished according to law. Simultaneously, it is naïve (and ineffective as well) to ignore the basic forces that give rise to the lawbreaking. In the area of business contributions to the political process, much of the basic thrust comes from the great power that—

through the political process—government has been given over business, power that ranges from awarding contracts and subsidies to withholding approval of new products and facilities.

The Prospects for Another Wave of Government Regulation

The current national debate on the role of government power and regulation is taking place on two distinct tiers. On one level, there is growing interest in applying cost-benefit analysis to regulation, in giving Congress veto power over individual regulations, and other procedural changes. The proponents of regulatory programs often oppose any of these changes in the belief that they would weaken the programs. The measures that are adopted are likely to be marginal. Some intermediate position provides the most realistic outcome, such as a continuation of existing federal regulatory activities although their administration may involve a bit more economic rationality.

Simultaneously, an effort is under way which in effect would leapfrog the entire current generation of regulatory activity. The second approach is in terms of a more basic expansion in governmental influence on private sector decision-making by means of establishing a formal system of national economic planning. In recent years, the federal budget and the annual economic report of the President have been used as vehicles for presenting broad-gauge and long-term projections of future economic conditions and of national priorities, at least to the extent that the changing allocation of federal monies indicates revisions in the relative importance of the major program and policy areas.

Increasing attention is being given to specific proposals such as the Humphrey–Javits and Humphrey–Hawkins bills, which would augment and focus the power of the federal government in an attempt to reduce unemployment substantially and to attain other important national objectives. A stock argument used by the proponents of these bills is that if private industry does long-range planning, why can't the government do the same? The short answer is that the national government doing the planning for the American people would not be the same thing as individual private organizations doing their own planning.

There are fundamental differences between business planning and government planning. In essence, we are dealing with the difference between forecasting and reacting to the future, and trying to control it. Corporate planning of necessity is based on attempting to persuade the public to purchase the goods and services produced by a given firm. The controls that may accompany the plan are internally oriented. In striking contrast, the government is sovereign. Its planning ultimately involves coercion, the use of its power to achieve the results it desires. Its controls are thus externally oriented, extending their sway over the entire society.

The proponents of a formal national economic planning system say that they would not set specific goals for General Motors, General Electric, General Foods, or any other individual firm. But what would they do if these companies did not conduct themselves in the aggregate in accordance with the national plan? Would they leave the actual results to chance or to the free market? Hardly. The Initiative Committee for National Economic Planning states that the planning office "would try to induce the relevant industries to act accordingly."[9] And the inducements are not trivial. The government's powers to tax, to purchase, to subsidize, to "assist," and to regulate are awesome. The most powerful planning system in the private sector lacks the ability to levy taxes.

Much of the rhetoric favoring a centralized economic planning system is phrased in terms of merely developing better information. But even a cursory examination of the literature on American business planning demonstrates that planning is intended to be far more than improved information accumulation. A standard definition is: "A plan is a predetermined course of action . . . to accomplish a specific set of . . . objectives."[10] One expert offers the most terse rendition: "Planning is to a large extent the job of making things happen that would not otherwise occur."[11] The proponents of centralized government planning do not leave the matter in any doubt. They clearly state: "The heart of planning is to go from information to action."[12]

The essence of the difference between public and private planning is

[9] "For a National Economic Planning System," *Challenge*, March–April 1975, pp. 52–53.

[10] Malcolm H. Sherwood, Jr., "The Definition of Planning," in *Readings in Business Planning and Policy Formulation*, ed. Robert J. Mockler (New York: Appleton, 1972), p. 103.

[11] David Ewing, *Long-Range Planning for Management* (New York: Harper, 1964), p. 3.

[12] "For a National Economic Planning System," p. 52.

the locus of decision-making. If Ford or Chrysler or General Motors are not selling as many automobiles as they had planned, there are a limited number of things they can do about it. They can, within their available resources, lower the price or change the nature of the product; but (as evidenced by the demise of the Edsel, the LaSalle, and the DeSoto) they may simply be forced to abandon the project. The consumer remains the ultimate decision-maker.

The situation is far different in the public sector. If the government does not believe that the American public is buying enough cars, it can lower the price as much as it likes via tax reductions. It can subsidize the private manufacture of automobiles or simply take over the ownership of the industry.

My point is not that private planning does not involve control, but that those subject to its control powers are very different. Once a private corporation adopts its long-range plan, it may push hard on the various units of the corporation to meet their goals and objectives. But the controls are internal—incentives and sanctions focusing on the officers and employees of the corporation. If things go wrong, the onus falls on them. Government planning, in contrast, focuses on "guiding" or "influencing," and thus ultimately controlling, the activities of the entire nation. If things go wrong in public sector planning, it will be the taxpayers and consumers who bear the burden.

Two types of government planning need to be distinguished: The external planning, which is discussed here, involves all sorts of extensions of government powers over the private sector. A second type of government planning is more internally oriented and is comparable to private sector planning. It relates to the management of government's own activities. In advocating national planning, Senator Hubert Humphrey deals with this second aspect:

the manner in which we are presently utilizing government resources and government agencies is a haphazard, helter-skelter enterprise. . . . We can show that with some planning in our government, just a modest amount, a little more than we're doing, we can reduce government costs and get better governmental services.[13]

[13] "Planning Economic Policy, An Interview With Hubert H. Humphrey," *Challenge*, March–April 1975, p. 23.

Perhaps a government being conducted on such a haphazard, helter-skelter basis should not be given the extremely ambitious task of managing the entire economy prior to getting its own house in order.

A comprehensive scheme of national economic planning could shift the focus of private enterprise even further away from dealing with market forces and meeting consumer demands and toward reaching an accommodation with an ever more powerful governmental bureaucracy. The payoff from traditional consumer market research might be less than from new efforts to persuade the government to adopt more generous production targets for an industry.

We could readily conjure up visions of civilian companies following some of the practices of that branch of American industry, defense production, which is now most closely tied to governmental decision-making. Business-financed hunting lodges and fishing trips for civilian government planners might seem to merely follow an older defense-industry tradition. But such public sector "marketing" activities would be a low-priority use of business resources. Yet, given the incentive of any organization to try to prosper in the environment it faces, this result would not be surprising under a system of strong national economic planning.

The advocates of centralized planning who base their case on an extension of business planning activities also overestimate the state-of-the-art in the private sector. No amount of formalized planning has eliminated any company's uncertainty concerning future technological change, the vagaries of weather, discoveries of energy or other natural resources, outbreaks of war, assassinations of national leaders, or shifts in the desires of the fickle consumer. Even discounting the shortcomings of existing business planning techniques, the differences between business and government decision-making are fundamental.

Business planning is based on the traditional assumption that individual consumers make the ultimate decisions on the allocation of resources in society. An important corollary is that if a company guesses wrong on what consumers buy it will suffer the consequences.

Government planning is based on an intrinsically different set of assumptions. Government determines what it considers to be in the society's overall interests. If the public does not respond accordingly, it is

not the planners who are considered to be at fault. Rather, new and more
effective devices are developed to get the public to accommodate to
the planners' view of the good (or great) society. The greatest danger of
adopting centralized planning is that it will, perhaps unintentionally at
first but inevitably as its initial results prove disappointing, propel our
country toward greater government control over individual behavior.

Reforming the Regulatory Process

Numerous bills have been introduced in Congress to reform one or
more aspects of the process of governmental regulation of business activities. Some would "deregulate" specific industries, notably railroads and
airlines, by dismantling a portion or all of the control apparatus established by the old-line regulatory commissions. Other approaches are
in terms of compulsory periodic reviews of each major regulatory program, designed to determine whether it is worthwhile in the light of
changing circumstances. Most of these "sunset" bills do not provide any
objective criteria to guide the presidential and congressional reviews
that would be required.

Many economists favor another route, which essentially is complementary and not competitive with the more legalistic approaches. It is to
urge that cost-benefit calculations be required in the governmental regulatory process as a means of correcting the various shortcomings that I
have described. Specific proposals have been made to limit the promulgation of new regulations to those instances where it can be demonstrated that the benefits to society will exceed the costs being imposed.
A greater emphasis on economic rationality surely is commendable,
even after allowances for the limitations of the state of the art of cost-
benefit estimation.

Moving beyond questions of mathematical measurement of the gains
and losses from government intervention, there is a strong case for
"economizing" on the power granted to governmental agencies. The evidence is in the main anecdotal, but some of the individual episodes illuminate strikingly the use of this power, an aspect of regulation that
cannot be discerned in the more conventional and statistical evaluations
that economists prefer to make.

A new way of looking at the microeconomic effects of government programs is needed. A parallel can be drawn to macroeconomic policy-making, where important and at times conflicting objectives are recognized. Attempts at reconciliation or trade-offs are made, such as among economic growth, employment, income distribution, and price stability. At the programmatic or microeconomic level, it is also necessary to reconcile the goals of specific government programs with other important national objectives; this mediation is not in practice a concern of many governmental agencies. In part, this reconciliation needs to occur at the most basic stages of the governmental process: when the President proposes and the Congress enacts a new regulatory program. In developing an environmental statute, for example, they need to keep in mind that a cleaner environment is not the only important need of the society, and that each increment of regulatory power reduces the extent of individual freedom and of private sector discretion. At the operating level, they, together with the administrators of the statute, need to understand that there may be more than one way of achieving the desired objective— and that the search for efficient solutions is not synonymous with a "green eyeshade" approach to social goals.

Some type of quantitative analysis, such as cost-benefit estimation, may play a useful role in that reconciliation process. But the policy-formation process needs to do more than produce another set of so-called inflation impact statements. First of all, the costs and the benefits of governmental actions need to be more than examined; they should be weighed against one another. In the process, the actual or proposed regulations that generate excessive costs should be modified or eliminated. But we need to go beyond the direct impact on price, and include the relationship to productivity, capital formation, and innovation. This decentralized approach to government policy would involve the setting of analytical and measurement standards for regulatory agencies by a unit that is not involved in conducting regulatory programs, such as the General Accounting Office or the Office of Management and Budget. That arm's length relationship is needed to assure uniformity in the measurements of benefits, costs, and other effects. Such standards would reduce the temptation of individual regulatory agencies to present self-serving justifications of their existing activities, albeit in a new economic framework.

Much would depend on the "teeth" that would be put into any

required economic-impact statement. Merely legislating the performance of some economic analysis by an unsympathetic regulator would primarily delay the regulatory process and make it more costly. But limiting government regulation to those instances where the total benefits to society exceed the cost would be a major departure. It could significantly slow down if not reverse the current trend toward federal regulation of business.

To an economist, government regulation should be carried to the point where the incremental benefits equal the incremental costs, and no further. (Indeed, this is the basic criterion which is generally used to screen proposed government investments in physical resources.) Overregulation, which can be defined as situations where the costs exceed the benefits, should be avoided. But if policy-makers tend to ignore or downplay the costs, we are bound to operate in the zone of overregulation, which is probably where we are today. In those cases where the benefits cannot be quantified in dollar terms, the approach could be a search for the least costly means of achieving the regulatory objectives. The existing literature on cost-effectiveness analysis can be drawn upon for that purpose.[14]

In choosing which regulations to adopt, the governmental decision-making body should give particular attention to several overhead areas that are often neglected: the monitoring costs of the government, the information costs imposed on both the public and private sectors, and the related private costs of compliance or avoidance. It is hardly coincidental that, simultaneous with the recent expansion of governmental regulatory activity, the cost of legal departments and of legal services has been one of the most rapidly growing segments of company budgets. In a different connection, Daniel Patrick Moynihan stated,

As government tries to do more, it will find it accomplishes less. That amounts to the discovery that administrative ability is not a free good, and in the absence of it the best intentioned programs can turn out to be calamities.[15]

[14] See Roland N. McKean, *Efficiency in Government Through Systems Analysis* (New York: Wiley, 1958); Charles J. Hitch and Roland N. McKean, *The Economics of Defense in the Nuclear Age* (Cambridge: Harvard, 1960).

[15] Daniel Patrick Moynihan, "The Future of Federalism," in U.S. Advisory Commission on Intergovernmental Relations, *American Federalism* (Washington, D.C.: Government Printing Office, 1975), p. 99.

It is important to build into the governmental processes those incentives which would encourage government officials to give greater weight to the costs and other side effects generated by the actions they take. Limiting new regulations to those instances where it can be demonstrated that net benefits accrue to society as a whole is one such device. At the operational level, attention might be given to the use of the budget process as an added tool for managing regulation. In those cases where an agency's regulations generate more costs than benefits, its budget for the coming year would be reduced, and vice versa. Another possibility for making the regulatory agencies more sensitive to the cost they impose on the society is for the Congress to give them "budgets" of private costs that they can cause to be incurred as the result of their regulations. Thus, an agency would be given not only a budget of X billion dollars for operating costs, but also Y billion dollars of social costs that it could incur during the year. In justifying their budget requests for those "social costs," the agencies would also be required to estimate the offsetting social benefits.[16]

The wide dissemination of the data on the economic impacts of government regulation might serve to alter the balance of interest-group forces now exerting pressures on the decision-making process. At present, it often appears that the interest groups which would benefit from the regulation are well aware of those positive contributions and thus mobilize their forces in favor of greater regulation. But the information on the adverse consequences of regulation, if widely distributed, might generate countervailing interest-group pressures.

More basically, however, it is attitudes that need to be changed. The experience under the job safety program provides a clear example. Although the government's safety rules, regulations, and requirements have resulted in billions of dollars in public and private outlays, the basic goal of a safer work environment has not been achieved.

A more satisfying answer requires a fundamental change in approach to regulation, and one that is not limited to the job safety program. Indeed, that program is used here merely as an illustration. If the objective of public policy is to reduce accidents, it should focus directly on the reduction of accidents. Excessively detailed regulations often are

[16] The author is indebted to Charles Holt of the Urban Institute for this suggestion.

merely a substitute for hard policy decisions. Rather than issuing cita-
tions to employers who fail to fill out the forms correctly or who do not
post the correct notices, the emphasis ought to be placed on those with
the worst safety records. (Variable insurance rates may perform a similar
function). As the accident rates decline toward some sensible average
standard, the fines could be reduced or eliminated.

The government should not be concerned with how a specific company achieves the objective of a safer working environment. Some may
find it more efficient to change work rules, others to buy new equipment, and still others to retrain workers. That is precisely the kind of
operational business decision-making that government should avoid but
that now dominates so many of these regulatory programs. Without
diminishing the responsibility of the employers, the sanctions under the
federal Occupational Safety and Health Act should be extended to employees, especially those whose negligence endangers other employees.
The purpose here is not to be harsh but to set up effective incentives to
achieve society's objectives. This can be a preferred alternative to government's specifying the details of "acceptable" private action.

Any realistic appraisal must acknowledge that important benefits have
resulted from many of the government's regulatory activities—in terms
of less pollution, fewer product hazards, reduced job discrimination, and
achievement of other socially desirable objectives of our society. It
should also be realized that Congress established these programs in
response to rising public expectations about corporate performance.

The "externalities" generated by federal regulation need not justify,
however, the government's attempting to regulate closely every facet of
private behavior. Indeed, the experience with existing governmental efforts indicates that further expansion of government involvement in the
detail of business decision-making is likely to be self-defeating. Rather,
some restraint might yield great rewards. Also, alternatives to regulation
need to be considered in adopting or improving public policy toward
business. In the environmental area, for example, selective taxes on certain forms of pollution may be a more effective and economical means of
achieving a given level of water quality than the promulgation of regulatory standards. In the case of industry-wide regulation, such as in transportation, greater reliance on competition may be a more effective way
of protecting the public interest. Utilizing a variety of approaches to

achieve the changes in business performance desired by public policy could also help to attain another important objective. The continued expansion of regulatory activities inevitably leads to a question that is difficult to answer, Who will regulate the regulators?

One obvious response is to suggest a general consolidation into a few or even one comprehensive agency which would provide a built-in mechanism for reconciling regulatory activities that now conflict. But, on reflection, such a concentration of governmental power may be cause for even greater concern. The dispersal of government power over a variety of regulatory, tax, and other activities—as well as greater reliance on private market forces—may be a promising alternative response to the accountability question.

The relationship between the government of a society and the members of that society is a delicate one, involving careful balancing of many important considerations. Clearly, the polar alternative of complete freedom is unrealistic. Anarchy is hardly a sensible response to the needs of a modern, high-technology society. Society does need to use the powers of government to help the individual members achieve objectives that they cannot attain on their own. It is generally acknowledged that government needs to set the basic rules for enforcing contracts, to provide for the national defense, and to deal with environmental and other "external" effects of individual behavior.

Yet, as we look around the world, it appears easy to move beyond that position to the undesirable situation where the state winds up directing the details of the day-to-day lives of the individual members of society. This is the other polar alternative, the totalitarian state.

I do not intend to close on the hysterical note that the United States is rapidly approaching a Big Brother–dominated society. But some words of caution do seem to be very much in order. We need to give much more attention to the delicate nature of the balance between the need for individual freedom and the desire to provide for the public welfare through government power.

Discussion

Quis custodiet ipsos custodes?

ROBERT LEKACHMAN. I will disagree with many of Murray Weidenbaum's conclusions in my own paper. One disagreement that must be taken up now, however, concerns the cost-benefit analysis that you associate with this "second managerial revolution." You argue that the regulatory powers of government have been extended in an excessive and often unintended manner. You condemn the costly use of political authority in a free economy, and you emphasize that the costs must largely be borne by risk-taking, entrepreneurial managers. But you say little about the social difficulties that regulatory agencies were supposed to correct.

Granting that the costs of control are as injurious as you suggest, you pay too little regard to demonstrable results: pharmaceutical products are safer, processed food is less impure, deceptive pricing is less pervasive, and consumer protection has been enhanced by these exercises in oversight. That business has been forced to negotiate over tougher standards is no bad outcome. Nor have the costs of upgrading product and safety standards been excessively burdensome, either to industry or to consumers. Moreover, since a significant number of jobs were created as a by-product, it is not necessarily inflationary to act vigorously in order to preserve a healthier social environment.

DAVID APTER. I am struck by the extent to which your analysis confirms, even if inadvertently, the Schumpeter analysis of change in capitalist society. You demonstrate that a dislocation of market procedures has emerged from closer government surveillance and the forceful surfacing of hidden social costs. But there is no cause for surprise. Schumpeter predicted that dislocation would result from the process of change. His thesis was confirmed when regulators tried to enforce free competition in uncompetitive industries, or when they reinforced consumer sovereignty in a supposedly free market system. The only surprise is that the private sector still accuses the government of ignoring social objectives and economic freedom. I find its case less than compelling.

This leaves unanswered critical questions about future behavior. Should we abandon or should we intensify the regulatory planning arrangements of the present day? Should we rationalize a better use of scarce resources, a better protection of social needs, and a better adaptation to technological change; or should we leave these decisions to the interplay of imperfect market forces? There are profound contradictions in our mixed economy. It is not demonstrable that they can best be resolved by curtailing the surveillance and the planning mechanisms of the public sector.

ROBERT GILPIN. There is another criticism that must be noted. It is argued that noncompetitive industries need to capture the single-purpose agencies that were set up, like the CAB or the ICC, to regulate their activities. These industries seek more public planning, not less, when it serves their interests or to protect their status as a "natural monopoly." It is claimed, in response, that AT&T has won few of its major disputes with federal antitrust authorities or with the rate-setting decisions determined by the states. But the fact remains that planning in the private sector has been stabilized by the intervention of public agencies; and this planning has helped protect great corporate interests.

CARL HORN. I must emphatically disagree with the assertion that regulated interests have in effect captured the regulators. Public agencies do not often share the goals and interests of private industries, whether they are in manufacturing or utility activities. Regulation is based on a retrospective analysis of past performance rather than on projections of future growth. It is not rational planning but irrational frustration that will result from a further extension of regulatory intervention. Public constraints provide little help in calculating the costs and benefits and the trade-offs facing risk bearing private capital. Neither will they secure an optimum use of national resources nor an improved planning for social efficiency.

RAYMOND VERNON. I am perplexed by this discussion of public sector needs, private interests, internal planning, and external constraints.

There are no common numerators against which we can measure social externalities or policy benefits. Nor is there good reason to pursue the mode of "indicative planning" that has been attempted in France. The planning ambitions of the Commissariat du Plan were abandoned in the sixth and seventh national plans. It now acts rather like the Council of Economic Advisors, as just another voice trying to gain the President's attention.

Reference has been made to the planning authority designated in the Humphrey–Hawkins bill. We should not exaggerate its potential impact. There will be numerous ways in which legal injunctions, bureaucratic initiatives, and political pressures can be mobilized to thwart its planning intentions. The U.S. political system is too fragmented to allow any rapid deployment of new planning powers.

Murray Weidenbaum suggests that we are in the midst of a revolutionary change of management; but Andrew Hacker concluded that this is not our historic period to institutionalize formal change. Given the contradictions in present trends, I can support neither hypothesis.

MURRAY WEIDENBAUM. Let me respond briefly. First, my comments on the capture of regulatory agencies are not original; both Milton Friedman and Ralph Nader have, surprisingly, agreed on this score. The experience varies from one federal agency or state public service commission to another. It is stronger in the case of the ICC and the CAB than the FCC. But the point that I made was that traditional, one-industry regulators are more sensitive to economic impacts than the planners who have established themselves in the executive departments. The latter deal with a single issue as it affects many industries and not with the sum of issues appearing in just one industry.

My second response: Of course I recognize the social benefits that have been gained by extending regulatory intervention. But think of the costs, too. Competent bureaucrats in the Food and Drug Administration have played it so safe that they have kept not only unsafe but also highly effective drugs from entering the market. In short, the relation of bureaucratic risks to rewards must be changed if we are going to loosen up the regulatory process. The extension of regulatory authority can impose prohibitive costs without securing appreciable social gains, whether in controlling food additives or in preserving the natural environment. If we shrink from criticizing the socially worthy agencies that safeguard equal opportunity or industrial safety when their rulings are too rigid or costly, we will generate few advantages for anyone in society.

Thirdly, there are strong advantages to be gained by using the price system or differential taxation, rather than regulatory controls, to move production from high- to low-pollution processes of manufacture. Similarly, there are stimulating incentives, not stringently written codes, that could reduce job hazards or automobile failures. The only test of the matter lies in the prevention of accidents or pollution discharges and not in the writing of new codes or the creation of new agencies.

FRANKLIN LONG. In short, what you recommend is that we distinguish between social responsibilities and opportunity costs. If herbicide manufacturers spend 35 percent of their R&D on defensive research, to guard against detrimental toxic effects, they should be encouraged as far as possible but compelled, if necessary, by regulatory fiat. That solution is acceptable so long as you accept two modifications: (1) managers in the private sector are often more reluctant to take risks than public agencies since their profit margins are at stake; and (2) public agencies have no right to expose the public to risk, as we found with thalidomide and aerosol sprays, so that greater profits can be reaped with untested R&D.

In whose benefit . . . Cui bono?

ELI GINZBERG. We have looked so far at the distribution between public and private sector responsibilities and between functional and regulatory controls. Clearly, there is a serious knowledge gap. The public sector can calculate its input costs (in salaries or support) but not its output. The private sector has better output information but we need to know more about its input. Is it beneficial to the U.S. economy if multinational firms relocate manufacturing jobs overseas; or if the giant banks and oil companies invest heavily abroad rather than at home?

Whether the interests of large corporations parallel those of an elected government is open to question. We do not have the data for a good answer. The best accountants work for private firms, and some of them put out remarkably irresponsible information. Justice Brandeis urged that the realities of private power had to be addressed in a civilized society.

It would be unwise to relax the regulatory power of government until
we know more about private power.

WALTER GOLDSTEIN. One of the central assumptions of our society is
that countervailing powers will strike a balance in the political and the
economic systems. If this is still correct, we should examine the com-
position as well as the constituency of the public bureaucracy. Sociol-
ogists looking for power elites have found government agencies staffed
by personnel on leave from (or en route to) the industries they regulate.
The practice is widely condoned on the grounds that government can
best acquire a data base by recruiting experienced specialists rather than
disinterested generalists into the ranks of the bureaucracy. As a result,
the best tax lawyers and accountants become experts at tax avoidance;
once they have been trained in the IRS, their skills are highly valuable
to the corporations that later hire them. There are fewer safeguards or
representatives for consumer interests in the present system.

So far the pressure of countervailing checks and balances has been
assessed in the need of private companies to stem the deployment of
new regulations. But two points remain to be made. First, deployments
are made after a tortuous, if not democratic, set of political procedures
were followed; few regulations were rushed into law before the pressurized
campaigns of interested lobbyists had run their course. Second, were it
not for the intervention of regulatory agencies, dominant forces in the
market might have come to acquire exorbitant power. The big three automobile companies represent the threat posed by any monopoly-run
industries. Drawing on vast advertising and lobbying budgets, they
campaigned first against the introduction of mandatory standards (for
better safety, gas mileage, or pollution controls) and then against the
recall of millions of cars that were demonstrably faulty. Was there any
possible countervailing force to Ford and GM but the slow, bumbling
measures of bureaucratic rule-writers?

MURRAY WEIDENBAUM. Rule-writing is not, itself, a danger. I favor
government controls on guns—and not on abortions. But I am suspicious of extensive bureaucratic requirements. To fulfill OSHA codes,
companies took professional safety personnel away from training workers
and had them fill out forms; as a result, occupational safety hazards were
not on balance reduced. Of all things, mistletoe was found to be an un-

safe product though no injuries have yet been attributed to it (unless kiss-
ing poses a health danger); but it may yet be ordered off the market.

I pointed out in my book, *The Modern Public Sector*,[17] that government is a limited resource. In terms of programs and regulatory codes,
we have probably long passed the limits of feasible operation. But we do
not know where to go from here. It will not help to build streamlined
superagencies, or to refine the quantity and quality of code writing.
Repeating the errors of the past will neither solve bureaucratic problems
nor ease the mounting tension between the public and private sectors.

A prize example of how *not* to operate can be drawn from the most
tightly controlled industry in our society. There is a regulatory docu-
ment known as the "Armed Services Defense Procurement Regulation."
Although it sets out defense procurement requirements in minute detail, Lockheed achieved a cost overrun of billions of dollars in building
the C-5ᴬ, and the wings of the F-111 kept falling off.

No industry should be expected to follow hundreds of pages of fine
print in planning its production schedules, nor is anything gained by
forcing managers to do so. Economizing in controls and slimming down
the bureaucratic apparatus will do more to fulfill societal objectives than
adding copious details to the code books. Admittedly, a move toward
deregulation will not safeguard us against the scandal of a kepone decision, but it will secure valuable advantages for our pluralist economy.

WALTER GOLDSTEIN. I am uneasy about proposals for deregulation or
self-regulation. If the first were followed, the vacuum left by federal
deregulation might be filled by aggressive but fragmentary reactions on
the part of states and municipalities. The problems of bureaucratic duplication and slipshod decision-making would then be compounded, not
eased. The second recommendation, for self-policing in the private sector, is equally unconvincing. It would allow oligopoly firms to charge
whatever the traffic would bear rather than what the economy required.
Moreover, if an organization as massive as AT&T were asked to police
its own natural monopoly, it would be subjected to acutely politicized
argument. The externalities of deregulation might in fact appall the most
conservative of contemporary critics.

[17] New York, Basic Books, 1969.

RICHARD WILSON. I agree that the deregulation of the telecommunications industry would hinder AT&T more than it would help. The same is true for other utility companies trying to achieve greater economies of scale in operation. There is always a danger, of course, that the regulators will be captured by the regulated, as has been noted. But it would be worse if the regulators were no longer fully informed about the industry which they were charged to supervise.

The other side of the equation must not be overlooked, however, in this survey of future action programs. The FCC could enhance its public accountability, for example, by adhering more closely to the Communications Act of 1934. Since 1968 the FCC has departed from its congressional mandate by imposing its own prescriptions for competition. This has threatened the Bell System's capability to provide nationwide service, particularly in rural areas or small towns where operations can be very costly. If the FCC allows competitors to selectively price AT&T out of markets where costs are on the low side of averages, what will happen to our system responsibilities? We cannot follow the example of the Post Office and close down rural facilities or suspend uneconomic activities. Improving the accountability of public agencies, therefore, might provide a better answer than deregulation.

MURRAY WEIDENBAUM. The point is well taken. In my paper I criticized the extension of new regulations, across several industries, not the traditional surveillance of telephone, gas, or electric utilities. These are natural monopolies and they require sensitive oversight.

But in a nonmonopoly industry, such as trucking, the ICC has set up barriers to new entries. This particularly hurts new, small, or minority enterprises. Self-regulation in this instance would provide a better answer than myriads of ingenious codes or control mechanisms. Trucking is only one of the examples that could be cited where both social objectives and effective planning are defeated by an overzealous resort to regulatory instruments. Hence, the conclusion of my paper: in this second managerial revolution we must pay closer attention to the delicate balance between the private and public uses of power.

NATIONAL PLANNING AND THE MULTINATIONAL ENTERPRISE

The U. S. Case

RAYMOND VERNON

National Planning and Transnational Interests

ONE OF THE EXTRAORDINARY DEVELOPMENTS of our century has been the deepening and strengthening of the idea that the modern state has a responsibility to actively promote the well-being of ordinary people. The idea itself came out of the revolutions of the eighteenth and nineteenth centuries, gaining in vigor as the modern industrial economy emerged and as national governments increased their capacities to tax, to regulate, to manage, and to spend.

Meanwhile, giant advances in communication, transport, and travel succeeded in bringing the remote corners of various national territories into closer contact. In Europe and North America, the railroads, canals,

Raymond Vernon is the Herbert F. Johnson Professor of International Business Management at the Graduate School of Business Administration and director of the Center for International Affairs at Harvard University.

and highways helped create national markets, national enterprises, national labor unions, and national mass political parties.[1] After the First World War, high tariffs and foreign exchange licensing gave added economic meaning to national borders. The limits defined by those borders took on still greater significance as a system of private international cartels appeared which generally used national boundaries to divide world markets among the rivals from different nations.[2]

At the outbreak of World War II, with national economies well delineated, the concept of the activist welfare state was still gathering strength. Nevertheless, one of the very forces that had helped the idea toward realization seemed already to become an obstacle. The persistent advances in transport and communication that over the preceding century had helped knit together the internal national markets of the United States, France, Germany, and Italy were now beginning to link these states more closely to one another. The international telephone, the commercial aircraft, and the computer began to widen the field of observation and action for businesses, professions, political movements, and consumers. From the viewpoint of New York or Washington, San Francisco was no longer much closer than London and Rome.

After World War II, these technical advances were matched by institutional changes that added to the widening of horizons. The U.S. government led a movement to reduce tariffs, trade quotas, and licensing of foreign exchange transactions among the leading industrialized countries. The International Monetary Fund, the General Agreement on Tariffs and Trade, and the Organization for Economic Cooperation and Development were some of the tangible consequences. Technological change and institutional change combined to produce a striking increase in the international flow of goods, money, ideas, and people.

[1] T. C. Cochran and W. E. Miller, *The Age of Enterprise: A Social History of Industrial America* (New York: Macmillan, 1942); G. R. Taylor, *The Transportation Revolution 1815–1860* (New York: Rinehart, 1951); Carter Goodrich, et al., *Canals and American Economic Development* (New York: Columbia Univ. Press, 1961); Albert Fishlow, *American Railroads and the Transformation of the Antebellum Economy* (Cambridge: Harvard Univ. Press, 1965).

[2] See, for instance Ervin Hexner, *International Cartels* (Chapel Hill: Univ. of North Carolina Press, 1946); G. W. Stocking and N. W. Watkins, *Cartels in Action* (New York: Twentieth Century Fund, 1946); and L. G. Franko, *The European Multinationals* (London: Harper, 1976), pp. 84–98.

In the three decades following 1945, international trade grew at a rate that was measurably faster than the growth of world output.[3] By 1975, U.S. exports had risen to over 7 percent of the country's gross product and, perhaps more significantly, to nearly 15 percent of the movable goods generated in the nation during that year.

Scholars and journalists have repeatedly stressed that during the years following World War II the United States also came to rely more and more on foreign sources for basic raw materials, including oil and non-ferrous metals. As long as the materials came from diversified foreign sources and as long as those sources found it hard to unite in some joint strategy, the United States' increased reliance did not necessarily imply an increased exposure to external influences. But it did open up a possibility, which later would become a reality, that foreign suppliers could pool their bargaining power and increase the vulnerability of the U.S. economy.

Perhaps as telling an exposure to other economies, however, has been the increase in another kind of international trade: the increase in both U.S. exports and U.S. imports of relatively sophisticated products: machinery, chemicals, automobiles, electronics, and so on.[4] These are highly differentiated items, quite unlike the timber, oil, wheat, and coffee beans that historically had accounted for the bulk of world trade. They demanded the creation of elaborate transnational networks through which effective communication, distribution, and maintenance operations could be conducted. As a result, foreign involvement in the U.S. economy and American participation in foreign economies took on a new quality of continuity and commitment.

The financial links between the U.S. economy and the economies of other countries also expanded greatly. By 1975, U.S. banks had outstanding loans to foreigners of about $30 billion and outstanding deposits from foreigners of about $24 billion, both figures being two or three

[3] See, for instance, General Agreement on Tariffs and Trade (GATT), *International Trade 1974/1975* (Geneva, 1975), p. 2; also R. N. Cooper, *The Economics of Interdependence* (New York: McGraw-Hill, 1968), pp. 59–63; Assar Lindbeck, "The Changing Role of the Nation State," *Kyklos* 28 (1975): 28–46.

[4] See, for instance: Organization for Economic Cooperation and Development (OECD), *The Chemical Industry, 1967–1968* (Paris, 1968), pp. 35–37; OECD, *Policy Perspectives for International Trade and Economic Relations* (Paris, 1972), p. 147; and General Agreement on Tariffs and Trade (GATT), *International Trade, 1967* (Geneva, 1968), pp. 31–75.

times as high as they had been a decade earlier.[5] During that period, the leading U.S. banks learned how to use their overseas subsidiaries to collect dollars on their behalf in European capital markets whenever money was scarce at home, and to loan dollars overseas when money was plentiful at home.

The proliferation and strengthening of the links between the U.S. economy and foreign economies could also be seen in the heightened ambition of American firms to secure foreign patents, as well as the greater interest of foreigners in securing American patents. In 1972, the U.S. Patent Office was issuing 31 percent of its new patents to foreigners, compared with only 13 percent in 1955. During the same period, U.S. nationals had increased their share of the patents being issued by other countries; their share of German patents, for instance, rose from 6 percent in 1955 to 22 percent in 1972. Accordingly, the linking of the American economy with others in intricate webs of commitment developed over a wide front.

The Multinational Enterprises

The emergence of the multinational enterprise as a major force in international trade and investment was greatly helped by technical advances in transport and communication. Scattered examples of the multinational structure have appeared throughout the century or so since modern industry first made its appearance in the United States.[6] Here and there, firms with headquarters in the United States established branches and subsidiaries abroad and learned to manage the various units of their international network pursuant to some common strategy, using the capital, knowledge, and experience of the network as a whole to support any of its parts. After World War II, however, the trend accelerated greatly. Contributing to it was the fact that, as the international links in communication were improved, national variations in

[5] Federal Reserve Board, reproduced in A. F. Brimmer and F. R. Dahl, "Growth of American International Banking: Implications for Public Policy," *Journal of Finance* 30, no. 2 (May 1975): 345.

[6] Mira Wilkins, *The Emergence of Multinational Enterprise* (Cambridge: Harvard Univ. Press, 1970); Charles Wilson, "Multinationals, Management, and World Markets: A Historical View," in *Evolution of International Management Structures*, ed. H. F. Williamson (Newark, Del.: Univ. of Delaware Press, 1975), pp. 193–216.

consumer tastes and national differences in industrial processes began to diminish. For the rich of all continents, the Mercedes and the skiing vacation became standard fare; for the very poor in all countries, plastic pails, aluminum roofing, and aspirin became items of universal consumption. For the income groups in between, the radio and television, the motorbike and compact car, Levi's and McDonald's hamburgers were symbols of the new universal norms. These homogenizing trends meant, among other things, that an enterprise which had learned to do something well on its own home turf could hope to use its experience and its knowledge successfully elsewhere.

At the same time, the great strides being taken in transport and communication produced powerful new economies of scale for some enterprises. Worldwide tanker and ore-carrying fleets, for instance, could be directed from a central control point and their movements integrated into processing plants operating all over the world. The difficulties that any organization would face in maintaining effective coordination and control over a network of units spread out to the earth's remoter corners declined, as computerized messages were sent with much reduced risks of error in the communicating network and greatly improved capacities for locating and retrieving vital information.

The conditions for the development of multinational enterprises were improved even further after the war by the reduction in national controls at the borders. The production facilities of American enterprise in different countries could be integrated into one effective planning unit, capable of supplying all the markets of the enterprise. When building such networks, enterprises could take advantage of large scale in the various stages of production where it existed and could exploit the different factor costs prevailing in the various economies. They could also diversify their sources of supplies and their markets, and gain the added stability and protection that went with such diversification.

At the end of World War II, both the tacit and the explicit market-sharing agreements that had existed between the leading U.S. firms and their European counterparts in many branches of industry were beginning to break down. These agreements had existed widely in chemicals, machinery, electrical equipment, metals, and petroleum, the very industries in which multinational enterprises were to grow most rapidly. A series of antitrust suits, launched in the early 1940s, began to have their effects.[7] Besides, even where suits were not being pressed, U.S. firms saw little reason for maintaining restrictive market-sharing agreements with European or Japanese firms or entering into new agreements of this sort. Debilitated by the effects of the war, these foreign firms were temporarily out of the international running, being short of capital, behind in technology, and preoccupied with the problems of their home markets.

With their competitors enfeebled, U.S. firms began to push into markets that had previously been dominated by the Europeans and the Japanese. American exports of a considerable number of industrial products increased spectacularly; by 1950, exports of trucks, agricultural machinery, electrical machinery, and iron and steel manufactures had all increased at least fourfold over prewar levels.

Alongside the increase in exports went the establishment of U.S.-owned producing subsidiaries in foreign markets. Sometimes U.S. firms set up subsidiaries to serve markets that had previously been supplied by exports; but at other times U.S. firms created or acquired such subsidiaries as a base for their first penetration of foreign markets.[8] In any case, by the mid 1970s, most large U.S. firms had substantial operating facilities located in foreign countries.

From the viewpoint of the United States, the trend had profound effects. In 1950, the big U.S. firms that could be regarded as multinational, when taken in the aggregate, accounted for only 17 percent of total sales in the industrial sector of the economy. By 1967, however, big firms that could be classified as multinational were responsible for 42 percent of total industrial sales in the United States. And by 1974, the firms then classified as multinational were accounting for 62 percent of aggregate U.S. industrial sales.

By the 1970s, too, the commitment of large U.S.-based firms to their foreign producing subsidiaries was considerable. A group of 179 such U.S. firms, for example, reported that in 1974 their foreign manufacturing subsidiaries had accounted for nearly $200 billion of sales, a figure

---

[7] Summarized in Kingman Brewster, Jr., *Antitrust and American Business* (New York: McGraw-Hill, 1958), pp. 26–36.

[8] For a detailed description of the process, see my book *Sovereignty at Bay: The Multinational Spread of U.S. Enterprise* (New York: Basic Books, 1971), chapter 3.

that compared with the group's U.S. sales of $340 billion.[9] The foreign contribution was especially striking in firms whose principal activity was in motor vehicles, drugs, oil refining, and chemicals.

Although the multinationalizing trend was especially apparent in U.S. industry during much of the postwar period, European and Japanese firms soon recovered sufficiently to choose the same options. Of course, some firms in Britain, Holland, Switzerland, and Sweden already had developed their own multinational networks dating back to the prewar period; these included such well-known firms as SKF, ICI, CIBA, and Shell. And the Japanese, although still far behind in the creation of multinational enterprises on the U.S. and European models, were in a position to build such structures out of their ubiquitous trading companies, already well established in many foreign markets.

At first, the European firms concentrated their multinational expansion in other parts of Europe, while the Japanese firms set up their foreign facilities in Asia. Eventually both the Europeans and the Japanese began to establish manufacturing facilities in the United States. By 1975, European and Japanese firms had made direct investments of nearly $10 billion in such activities.[10]

The motivations of these firms in establishing subsidiaries in the United States suggests that their commitment to the U.S. economy is not ephemeral.

In some cases, the decision has been based on simple cost calculations. Having developed a U.S. market by way of exports from the home base, some European and Japanese firms have calculated that their delivered costs to the U.S. market could be reduced by setting up a production unit here. The decline in the value of the dollar in the late 1960s and 1970s tipped the balance even a little farther in favor of setting up a producing U.S. subsidiary. Calculations of this sort underlay the decisions of Volvo, Volkswagen, and Sony, among many others, to set up production facilities in the United States.

In other cases, however, the decision has been based on defensive factors. Some European firms have worried that unless they set up a

[9] These data were compiled by the Harvard Multinational Enterprise Project.

[10] "Benchmark Survey of Foreign Investment in the U.S., 1974," *Survey of Current Business* 56, no. 5 (May 1976): 35–51.

U.S. subsidiary they would receive no effective stimulation from the challenges of the U.S. market; and, lacking stimulation, they might be handicapped when competing with the Americans in other markets. This was one of Unilever's reasons for its early initiative of setting up a U.S. subsidiary, and the same was true for Olivetti.[11]

Still other European and Japanese firms have felt the need to create a subsidiary in the United States partly as a counter to the U.S.-owned subsidiaries located in their main markets at home; according to the hypothesis, with each side capable of challenging the other in its main market, the probability of uninhibited competition would be reduced. That calculation apparently was what spurred Royal Dutch Shell to set up a U.S. subsidiary in 1910 to counteract the Standard Oil Company's intrusions abroad, and it is thought to have contributed decades later to the similar decisions of Pechiney, BASF, and British Petroleum.[12]

The upshot is that enterprises organized on a multinational scale have come to account for a considerable proportion of the economic activity of the United States, as well as for a dominant part of the flows of money and funds across its national borders. The U.S. planner, like many planners in Europe, must contemplate the disconcerting fact that most of the producing facilities in his own country are attached to a global network extending into many other markets. This perception will substantially affect the planner's goals, his preferred instrumentalities, and his perception of the planning risks. Before exploring these effects, however, I wish to review some of the attributes that characterize U.S. planning, stressing especially those aspects that bear on the multinational enterprise.

Planning, American Style

Ten or fifteen years ago, the term national planning began to acquire a fairly explicit technical meaning. Although nations did not necessarily agree on the means to be used for achieving any set of planning goals, considerable agreement did exist on how planning objectives were to be

[11] See *Sovereignty at Bay*, p. 111.

[12] E. M. Graham, "Oligopolistic Imitation and European Direct Investment in the United States," unpublished D.B.A. thesis, Harvard Business School, 1974.

specified and how the inputs needed for achieving the specified objectives were to be determined.

The goals to be sought were defined as a rule in national economic aggregates: in jobs, income, output, savings, and investment. A national input/output matrix was needed for these goals to be measured and specified. Imports were generally seen as inputs of last resort, to be undertaken only for products that were required by the plan but that the national economy could not provide. The amount of exports was determined by the foreign exchange needed for the imports. Domestic savings, it was assumed, would be used in the first instance at home, not in foreign countries. Foreign savings would be used to deal with any shortfall.

How all these targets were to be achieved depended on the preferences of the country engaged in the planning exercise. The open market might be allowed a role; indeed some considerable part of the plan might be no more than a projection of the results that the open market would be expected to generate. Somewhere in the picture, however, conscious intervention would presumably have to occur if specific planning goals were to be achieved. Some of the needed intervention was almost sure to take place at the national borders, in the form of import or export restrictions, import or export subsidies, or changes in the exchange rate. Intervention could also take place inside the country, whether through the public sector's investment and production program or through monetary and fiscal policy, or through exhortation and regulation of the private sector.

That approach made some sense in its time; but its time was the 1950s, not the 1970s. In the 1950s, outside of the socialist world, France and Japan were the most advanced in the practice of national planning. For the two of them, the conditions implicit in the specification of a national plan along the lines just described were not wholly unrelated to reality. The problem of both countries at the time was to fill an elastic demand, given a constraint on some of the critical inputs, including foreign exchange. Among the instruments available to them was the imposition of restrictions at the border. But those conditions rapidly faded during the 1960s, and by the 1970s both the national goals and the international environments for achieving those goals had been profoundly altered. Any industrialized country that was thinking seriously about planning, including the United States, would have to take these changes into account in formulating its national planning exercise.

The first such change has been the increase in importance of foreign transactions to the national economy. Neither France nor Japan nor even the United States is any longer quite so free to consider imposing restrictions on cross-border transactions in order to further some national plan. During the 1960s both France and Japan were forced to confront the fact that their respective economies had grown increasingly dependent on sustained access for their products to the markets of other countries. The need for continuous access stemmed from many factors. One was the growing importance of scale in modern industry. In some industries, the need for increased scale showed up in the size of the programs that were required for the development of new products or processes; this was the case, for instance, in aircraft, nuclear reactors, office machinery, and drugs. In other industries, such as food products and automobiles, distribution and marketing requirements pushed enterprises to greater size. In still other industries, including aluminum and chemicals, the size factor showed up strongly in the production stage.

Besides, the growing sophistication of the products being offered in international markets required producers to maintain much tighter control over distribution networks, trade names, and maintenance facilities in foreign countries, as well as to maintain continuous contact with the technologies being generated by others.

Once the foreign trade of a nation began to contain significant quantities of products of that sort, the flow could not be turned off except at great cost. Accordingly, foreign trade could no longer be treated as external to the national economy, to be used only as necessary to dispose of surpluses and to cover shortages. National planners thereby lost some of their power to regard the foreign sector as an element external to the national plan.

For U.S. planners, the foreign trade and foreign payments of the country have grown in importance in relation to the national economy. But what matters as much or more is the fact that over 60 percent of U.S. industrial output is accounted for by firms that have a substantial network of overseas producing subsidiaries. Any national plan has to be drawn so as to take these networks into account, both for their capacity to pick up and broadcast the tremors generated in the rest of the world and for their capacity to broadcast the shocks and variations originating in the United States.

The realization of national planners in different countries that their respective bailiwicks were becoming interlinked in disconcerting ways was one of the important factors that led in the early 1970s to the abandonment of the fixed exchange-rate regimes that for twenty-five years had been sanctified by the International Monetary Fund. Flexible exchange rates were introduced on the assumption that such rates would allow national authorities to maintain some degree of control over the national economy without having to shut off transactions with the rest of the world.

The reasons why flexible rates were thought to give greater autonomy to the national authorities are technical and complex. In a system of flexible rates, it was thought, the public's expenditures on foreign exchange would be equal to the public's acquisitions of foreign exchange, and the effect of the foreign sector on the national money supply would accordingly be neutral. The hope was that once national authorities were relieved of the obligation to intervene in the foreign exchange market, they would be free to use the tools of monetary policy in the pursuit of national goals.

After half a decade of experience with flexible exchange rates, it is clear that governments have not succeeded in throwing off the problems of their pervasive monetary interdependence. Contrary to expectation, the Federal Reserve Board finds itself deeply enmeshed in transactions in the foreign exchange market; cyclical movements in the U.S. economy still broadcast their effects into the other economies; changes in the prices of key commodities spread quickly across the exchanges; large supplies of liquid funds continue to flood into and out of the country, in pursuit of security as well as profit.[13] In short, the open borders of the country continue to limit the U.S. planner's capacity to take the foreign environment as given and to concentrate his attention on the national turf alone.

Another factor that could well condition the U.S. approach to plan-

---

[13] See, for instance, W. M. Brown, *World Afloat: National Policies Ruling the Waves*, Essays in International Finance, no. 116 (Princeton: Princeton University, May 1976).

ning is the striking differences of view among the nation's leading economists over how the nation's economy works. It may be more than coincidence that in the countries where national planning has been seriously attempted, notably France and Japan, the nation's planners have not exhibited many large doctrinal differences over how the national economy operates. For the United States, however, the extent of doctrinal consensus has been much smaller.

In the United States, the unraveling of a professional consensus became apparent in the 1930s, under the impact of a great depression and of Keynesian economics. During the 1960s, economists briefly nourished the illusion that they had learned how to "fine-tune" the national economy through the application of monetary and fiscal policy. But the extraordinary behavior of international markets and international prices in 1973 and 1974 brought questions of monopoly and oligopoly back to center stage. Today, some of the most influential U.S. leaders in the practice of economic policy have very little in common beyond their vocabulary. The consensual disarray among economists persists, and any well-articulated national plan in the United States is unlikely to command respect from more than a limited sector of the economic leadership of the country.

Just as difficult for the U.S. planner is the subtle change in national goals that has occurred since the 1950s and 1960s. Nations no longer are prepared to put an unconditional primacy on economic goals such as the growth in national income or the increase in national employment. Although targets such as these continue to lie at the heart of the planning exercise, the U.S. public seems inclined to trade off such goals at times for the achievement of other objectives. These other objectives include, for instance, maintaining a livable environment, creating job opportunities for minority groups, and developing mechanisms for citizens' participation in the governmental process.

Although goals such as these may come and go from one decade to the next, the emphasis in the United States on citizens' participation is likely to endure. The emphasis has been institutionalized in various laws such as the Freedom of Information Act[14] and in various court decisions that allow citizens' groups to sue government officials in order to compel

---

[14] See G. L. Waples, "The Freedom of Information Act: A Seven Year Assessment," *Columbia Law Review* 74 (June 1974): 895–959.

performance.[15] Planning, American style, is likely to be powerfully conditioned by that aspect of our national life.

In fact, the basic style of U.S. governance may well prove to be incompatible with national planning in any ordinary sense of the term. The U.S. governing process, it has long been recognized, has to be distinguished from that of most other democratic industrial states in important respects. According to one well-supported view, American society is caught up in "a perennial quest for a way of dividing, diffusing and checking power and preventing its exercise by a single interest."[16] The familiar U.S. system of checks and balances is designed to aid that process, as is the special constitutional protection extended to the press.[17]

In other respects, too, the United States presents a strong contrast to most industrialized countries, particularly to countries that have had some experience with national planning. Take the nature of political parties in the United States. Differences in ideology between the Democrats and the Republicans are not very wide, certainly not as wide as the characteristic party differences found in Europe and Japan.[18] But within each party a wide array of convictions exists, so wide that a single party is able to embrace both a George Wallace and a Birch Bayh.

The same point can be made regarding the government bureaucracy in the United States. Compared with Britain, France, Japan, Germany, or Italy, the U.S. bureaucracy is a diverse group with neither common training, common ideology, nor a common perception of role and function.[19] New leadership is brought into the bureaucracy by each new administration, and the leadership is recruited from all sorts of backgrounds, including law, business, accounting, teaching, and the military.

[15] R. B. Stewart, "The Reformation of American Administrative Law," *Harvard Law Review* 88, no. 8 (June 1975): 1667.

[16] Richard Hofstadter, *The Paranoid Style in American Politics and Other Essays* (New York: Knopf, 1966), p. 205. See also S. P. Huntington, "Political Modernization: America vs. Europe," *World Politics* 18, no. 3 (April 1966): 378–414.

[17] See Potter Stewart, "Or of the Press," *Hastings Law Journal* 26, no. 3 (January 1975): 631–37.

[18] See, for instance, L. D. Epstein, *Political Parties in Western Democracies* (New York: Praeger, 1967), pp. 193–98.

[19] See Henry Jacoby, *The Bureaucratization of the World* (Berkeley and Los Angeles: Univ. of California Press, 1973), pp. 26–85; J. A. Armstrong, *The European Administrative Elite* (Princeton: Princeton Univ. Press, 1973), pp. 201–23, 244.

Finally, U.S. business groups prove to be no more cohesive than the political parties or the bureaucracy. Although the evidence suggests that U.S. businessmen tend to share a common set of ideological values, the economic interests that any national business group represents are enormously diverse. Because of the structure and style of U.S. governance, the capacity of each such interest to promote its cause independently of the others is reasonably high. One result is that the government finds it exceedingly difficult to designate private instrumentalities to serve in some special relation to the public sector. This precludes the so-called chosen instrument approach so common in Europe and Japan.[20] The consequence has been that the U.S. government has been sharply limited in its range of instruments and techniques available for the execution of any national policy.[21]

A realistic view of national planning, American style, therefore has to recognize that it is likely to be a fairly limited exercise. The specialists may be permitted to grind out national projections, and these may well set new standards in sophistication, detail, and frequency. But, once the disparate interests of the economy have all been heard, the goals of any planning exercise no doubt will prove to be broad and platitudinous, and the instrumentalities of execution will be dilute and indirect.

Projections and Policies

Some sort of planning activity is likely to be undertaken, nevertheless. When it is, the openness of the U.S. economy will condition the exercise in various explicit ways.

The Projections

The very first step in the planning exercise is likely to be the development of the economy's performances. Given the restraints and the re-

[20] For characteristic struggles over the subject, see T. P. Murphy, "Technology and Political Change: The Public Interest Impact of COMSAT," *Review of Politics* 33, no. 3 (July 1971): 405–24; M. J. Peck and F. M. Scherer, *The Weapons Acquisition Process: An Economic Analysis* (Boston: Division of Research, Graduate School of Business Administration, Harvard University, 1962), pp. 324–61; "Why Lockheed Needs Another Rescuer," *Business Week*, 17 March 1975, p. 22.

[21] For an account of how these factors have operated in the international problems of the oil industry, see my article, "The Influence of the United States Government upon Multinational Enterprises: The Case of Oil," in *The New Petroleum Order*, ed. Antoine Ayoub (Quebec: Les Presses de l'Univ. Laval, 1976).

sources of the national economy, the question for the planner is to determine what national goals can be achieved; and, if all desired goals cannot be achieved simultaneously, what trade-offs exist among the various goals. Can price stability be traded off against employment? Can output be traded off against environmental control?

Questions of the foreign supply of products and the foreign demand for products will play a considerable role in the projection. The planner will be obliged to cast his planning net into the economics of the countries that are the principal markets as well as the principal sources of competition for the United States.[22] Then he will find that his pursuit of the foreign link leads back full circle to the U.S. economy itself; for the size and importance of the U.S. economy are bound to affect directly the business conditions in Canada, Western Europe, and Japan, as well as Mexico, Brazil, and other developing countries. Projection will require an iterative process, in which the projected performances of the various economies—each subject to its own constraints, its own sources of disturbance, and its own priorities—are folded into a mutually consistent outcome.

The problems of multinational projection are substantially increased by the fact that they involve the international movements not only of goods and services but also of capital and technology. There was a time when the movement of capital across international borders was sufficiently minuscule or sufficiently well controlled that it could be handled as an exogenous variable, not as a variable whose value was determined substantially from other parts of the projection. That is no longer the case; capital, it is clear, moves easily across the borders of the industrialized countries in response to relative changes in national credit needs.

That change in the structure of the leading industrial economies may complicate the projection exercise. Multinational enterprises that have units established in the world's principal markets can be presumed to have a fairly reliable grasp of comparative conditions in the various markets, and can be expected to respond rationally to those conditions. But rational behavior for multinational enterprises includes responses

[22] For a popular treatment of the projection process, see "Economic Forecasting: The International Dimension", *OECD Observer* no. 79 (January–February 1976): 17–21. For a more technical treatment, see R. J. Ball, ed., *The International Linkage of National Economic Models* (New York: American Elsevier, 1973).

that are quite at variance with the behavior of a classically competitive market. The industries most closely identified with multinational enterprises are oligopolistic in structure, dominated by a small number of very large firms. In contrast to any pattern that a competitive model would be likely to produce, the same industries account for the bulk of the investment flowing in both directions across the Atlantic. Leaders in such industries are obliged to keep a close eye on one another's moves, hoping to discourage any aggressive efforts to upset the competitive balance. In their efforts to maintain that sort of stability, the leaders are constantly trying to ensure that none is stealing a march on the others. That is partly why in recent years the Japanese and French planning authorities have been tolerant of (indeed, encouraged) overseas moves by their leading national firms.[23]

Investments on this pattern seem destined to grow. As they do, they will complicate the task of projection, since they will be influenced by the distinctive situation in each industry as much as by the general condition of the economy at large.

The problem of dealing with the idiosyncratic characteristics of individual industries is likely to trouble the projection exercises on other grounds as well. Picture the decisions that multinational enterprises are making today in the location of new facilities in such industries as oil, aluminum, copper, automobiles, and chemicals. The multinational enterprises are both the leaders and the targets in a complex struggle that involves many nations. Some of the factors in the struggle, such as political stability and oligopolistic rivalry, have already been mentioned. But other industry-specific factors also are involved, including the rate at which companies can generate an internal flow of funds, and the threats and blandishments that individual countries may use to get their share of industrial expansion. In oil, copper, and aluminum, for instance, it is a good guess that multinational enterprises are holding back from investing in Zambia, Libya, Peru, Zaïre, Jamaica, and other developing countries, and expanding their investments in North America beyond the levels that simple economic calculations might suggest. In automobiles

[23] M. Y. Yoshino, *Japan's Multinational Enterprises* (Cambridge: Harvard Univ. Press, 1976), pp. 53–59; France, Commissariat Generale du Plan, *Cinquième Plan de Développement Economique et Social 1966–1970* (Loi no. 65-1001, 30 Nov. 1965), p. 60; and *Sixième Plan* (Paris: Union Generale d'Editions, 1971) p. 16.

and chemicals, on the other hand, the governments of developing countries such as Mexico, Spain, and Brazil may be using their economic muscle to capture more than their economic share of the multinational enterprises' output. All this adds up to a difficult exercise for the projection specialists.

The Policies

From the viewpoint of national planners, projections are a preliminary to intervention; if the projections generate results that are unsatisfactory, then new public policies may be called for. I have already suggested that the public policies which the United States institutes in the name of planning are likely to be more reactive than aggressive. Generalized monetary and fiscal measures are more probable than specific measures aimed at well-delineated targets.

In a world of open international borders and multinational enterprises, however, the monetary and fiscal measures of any single country are unlikely to work very well unless coordinated with those of other countries. To be sure, the U.S. economy has a better chance than most for carrying out an independent monetary or fiscal policy. The sheer size of the U.S. economy may mean that leakages over the border will not wholly dilute the effects of such policies. But the experience of the industrialized countries ever since the mid 1960s suggests that the openness of national borders and the ubiquity of multinational enterprises have reduced the scope for independent national monetary and fiscal policies. The brief illusion that flexible exchange rates might allow open borders alongside of independent national policies has now been dispelled, and conflict once again seems inescapable.

The upshot is obvious, even trite. The industrialized countries seem to confront a choice among difficult alternatives. One is to restore national restrictions at the border. But that will seem costly to all the countries concerned, because it will oblige them to give up the various efficiencies that the open borders seem to have generated. The other is to harmonize their national actions in the field of monetary and fiscal policy sufficiently to compromise their disparate national interests.

For the present, the industrialized countries have rejected the first alternative and are still contemplating the implications of the remaining choice. The ongoing work of the OECD and the "summit" gatherings of prime ministers and presidents at Rambouillet and Puerto Rico are a reflection of that preference.

The progress achieved through such channels has to be counted as trivial, however, when measured against the need. And the difficulties of achieving much more progress seem disconcertingly formidable. The reasons are fairly evident. Monetary and fiscal policies deal with the core questions of domestic politics. They bear on inflation, employment, and income distribution. The harmonization of national policies in these key fields requires domestic political groups in different countries to find some way of compromising their interests with groups in other countries. When the conflict lies within the borders of a single state, the machinery for that sort of process is embodied in national parliaments, executive agencies, and the courts. When the conflict straddles national borders, the machinery for communication and reconciliation barely exists.

Yet the need to harmonize national policies in order to maintain open borders seems compelling. As nations are being pushed closer and closer together, that sort of need may prove even more powerful. Otherwise, nations may be faced with the alternative (assuming it is any longer a practical alternative) of shutting themselves off from one another. That is one way of synthesizing the international problems faced by the national planner.

Discussion

The Nation State and Global Firms

DAVID APTER. It might be useful to start by looking at the conflict between territorially based governments and globally mobile MNEs (multinational enterprises). Most nations are inflexible in their goals and political methods. They are anxious to arrest the outflow of investment funds, of credit balances, or repatriated dividends while still trying to maximize inflows of new capital, jobs, and export production. They enjoy remarkably few options to control their own industrial development in the light of the competitive rivalries to capture international trade. It seems that the ability of the MNE to break into host-country markets and financial sources could eventually undermine the capacity of the nation-state to control its own economic planning.

RAYMOND VERNON. The ability of the MNE to operate as an independent management unit, with its internal control of information and products, is more important to the nation-state's development than the MNE's impact on financial flows. The MNE generally provides an extension of skilled management systems and a unique packaging of technology and organizational experience. This makes it a more dynamic force than Lenin envisaged when he formulated his critique of imperialism. Lenin condemned the flow of capital into the natural resources, utilities, and banking of the colonial world; these transfers fulfilled the nineteenth-century concept of "implantation," and he explained them in terms of the surplus values of the imperial states.

Today the MNE operates in the manufacturing industries in which capital and technology are rapidly diffused. The chemical industries, for example, have accelerated the life cycle of products and they keep introducing new products. Historically, the thrust toward product innovation has been more significant than the winning of new markets; that explains to some degree why the MNE has grown faster than many domestic firms. It has excelled in product differentiation and innovation by relying on its internal sources of strength.

FRANKLIN LONG. It is important to distinguish between the technology or the capital needs of various MNEs in the manufacturing industries. At the lower end of technology in the chemical industries (such as paints, coatings, or inks), capital is generated in local markets overseas. But there is also a major flow of technology license fees and dividends back to the parent company at home. This behavior is not followed by the MNEs that manufacture electronics equipment or watches; they take advantage of the cheap wage economies of Southeast Asia to handle their labor-intensive subassembly operations. In their case, the technology of only one phase of production is located overseas; the components are then shipped back to the home company for final assembly and processing. This second pattern minimizes the MNE's risks, as it requires only a small investment in politically volatile countries; and the investment, if properly located, can lead to an appreciable increase in the return realized on the MNE's global capital.

RAYMOND VERNON. There are many types of product cycle and investment requirements. The oligopoly mode of competition created by many MNEs is beneficial to the overseas licensing of R&D in some industries. In others, basic product cycles (as in chemicals) can be extended by differential pricing policies. It is difficult to formulate a comprehensive taxonomy of MNE forms and functions. The forms and functions of investment vary widely across the world.

A question has been raised regarding the increasing hostility and the economic nationalism that has been encountered by the MNEs in recent years. Denunciations at the U.N. have been particularly strident; the LDCs (less-developed countries) have alleged that they have been exploited or stripped of some of their independent sovereignty by the MNEs. Many have claimed to be victims of a *dependencia* syndrome. It must be noted, however, that the greatest hostility has come from the LDCs that do their utmost to protect their own interests, to curb their import bills, to regulate the flow of capital, or to force incoming MNEs to accept a minority partnership in a joint venture with local equity.

It must also be emphasized that the world has never been hospitable to the MNE. Apart from a unique period between 1950 and 1970, when the pace of world trade was rapidly accelerating, nation-states have generally been anxious or suspicious about direct foreign investment. In a book that I edited, *How Latin America Views the U.S. Investor*,[24] the last sentence of the introduction read, "the awakening is ruder when the dreams have been sweet." We are now waking up once again to the difficulties that the MNE must overcome in doing business abroad. In many countries the business environment is extremely harsh. But by resorting to joint ventures, management contracts, and other compromises of their autonomy, the MNEs have continued to expand their activities. They will probably be more important in the 1980s than they are today.

Who will benefit from the operations in the LDCs, it is constantly asked. The answer depends upon the alternatives that are assumed. The first alternative to be assumed is that the Soviets or the Chinese will donate their capital and management to friendly LDCs. This has not worked well so far. In most cases the donors have supplied pieces of technology on the shelf that were available for transfer. But transferring outmoded technology is of little value to an LDC looking for export markets or competitive modes of production.

The second assumption is that the MNE will contribute both to its own benefit and to that of the host country. It must then be asked how the added dividend will be shared. Most of the MNE's benefits end up in the host economy, in the form of wages to labor or taxes to the government that would otherwise not be obtained. By contrast, the added tax revenue paid to the home government is slight, approximating $1 billion each year in the case of American MNEs. Similarly, the added payment to the managers and stockholders of the parent MNE is also slight in comparison to the wages and suppliers' bills paid by the overseas affilitate. The absolute gain to LDCs is therefore important.

The one group with a right to worry about the division of benefits is the U.S. labor force. It has seen jobs flow overseas, to its detriment, but it has also seen an expansion of hiring by the MNEs at home. There is no certainty that a ban on MNEs would produce a result that was more

[24] New York: Praeger, 1965.

rewarding. Economic protectionism might force U.S. business to stay at home but it might also diminish the stock of jobs at home. This caveat aside, labor does have a good reason for wrestling over the uncertain choices that it must now face. On the whole, I suspect that limiting the autonomy of the MNE will not contribute to full employment, price stability, or economic equity.

JACK KOTEN. I agree with your conclusion but I find your reasoning too negative. In pointing to the limited conflicts between national planners and the MNEs, you underestimate their positive contributions. In many parts of the world the American MNEs have helped raise the standard of living by creating job opportunities and improving local productivity. In doing so they have accomplished more than the United Nations in creating a one-world reality of development and progress.

RAYMOND VERNON. That conclusion is more convincing to Americans than to poorer nations, as it implies the preeminence of American values and business procedures. Canadian, Africans, or Asians tend to see the reality in a less comforting manner.

Although he died tragically in his thirties, Stephen Hymer wrote an eloquent exposition of the opposing point of view. As a radical economist and a Canadian, Hymer rejected the elite values which he associated with the expansion of the MNE. He did not applaud the success of Coca-Cola or Pepsi-Cola in persuading millions of impoverished Mexicans to consume soft drinks. He condemned the expectation that major decisions and profits should be concentrated in MNE headquarters while affiliate companies were sent out to toil at the periphery. That division of labor, he argued, did little to build one world or to advance the cause of development in many of the poor countries.

Dividing the Benefits of Economic Growth

SYLVIA HEWLETT. The *dependencia* syndrome is more important to the LDCs than has so far been granted. It is easy to recommend that the Mexican government should discourage all artificial drinks instead of discriminating against Coca-Cola or Pepsi-Cola. But this does nothing to eradicate the real problem: the tendency of the MNE to warp the development strategies and priorities of an impoverished LDC.

The consumer tastes of the LDC population or the profits remitted from their economy by the MNE are less important than the influence exerted by foreign managers in deflecting the LDCs' economic growth plans. The global reach of the MNEs is sufficiently powerful to inhibit state-run or domestic enterprises in many parts of the world. As a result, the goals of domestic expansion and import substitution are shoved aside. In their place the MNE pursues the improvement of its profit and market positions. The benefits of expansion are distributed with little sense of equity.

WALTER GOLDSTEIN. Three points have been established so far. First, that the U.S. economy is becoming more and more interdependent with global trade. Second, that the uneven benefits of economic development cannot be easily corrected. Third, that there are few viable alternatives to the modes of MNE expansion depicted by Ray Vernon. As a consequence, there are no radical objectives that can be identified by national planners to conserve either the economic autonomy or the political sovereignty of the nation-state, no matter whether it is a home or a host to the MNE.

I find these conclusions to be depressing and premature. Admittedly, the alternatives to the free-enterprise structures in the international economy are not very promising. But there remain too many political defects and social injustices in the international economy for us to resign ourselves to the fact that world trade is controlled by the profit venturing of the MNEs and comparable institutions. Too many people suffer from the free trade benefits enjoyed by the MNE.

Economic protection may prove in the future to be harmful and threatening, yet it can offer improverished people a modicum of control over their own destiny. Admittedly, intervention by the state, whether it appears in Japan or in India, tends to inhibit the free play of market forces and thus impedes what Professor Kindleberger has called the "international equalization of factor costs." It must be granted, too, that *étatisme* and economic protectionism reflect a resort to mercantilist ideology and trade-war maneuvering. But are we sure that these obstacles to entrepreneurial efforts are demonstrably worse in their consequences than the influence wielded within the LDCs by even the best of the "world citizens" among the MNEs? The terrible experiences of Chile or Guatemala can only strengthen one's doubts.

Ray Vernon compared the benefits to the host and the home countries; he found that the balance favored the host. If we compare costs, and particularly opportunity costs, I am not sure that the equation works out so well. In welcoming the new capital, technology, and employment that the MNE can bring, the host economy finds that its growth plans are deflected, its social priorities are aborted, and its political discretion becomes subject to the managerial decisions exercised by foreign interests. Canada, Puerto Rico, and Singapore, to name only three host cases, have been unhappy with the results. The home countries, too, have discovered the mixed blessings generated by "free-trade imperialism." Under the guise of meeting foreign competition, some of their largest manufacturing, energy, and banking corporations have moved assets overseas to suboptimize their profits and to minimize costs. In doing so they have drained some of the strength from the home economy by relocating jobs or value-added production.

In his new book, *U.S. Power and the MNC*,[25] Robert Gilpin has suggested that American firms might exact as heavy a toll from the U.S. economy as their counterparts levied from Britain in the late nineteenth century. Namely, in pursuing expansion overseas they siphoned off from the home market an appreciable amount of capital, employment, and economies of scale in manufacturing.

It is not easy to urge a return to protective tariffs, import quotas, restrictions on technology transfers, or the suppression of capital outflows. These are dangerous protectionist measures to adopt in a world of interdependent nation-states suffering from resource shortages, unstable currencies, and inadequate growth. Clearly, the beggar-thy-neighbor tactics of trade warfare could produce negative-sum consequences for all nations, home and host countries alike. But so, too, can the alternative system that Ray Vernon describes. If the MNEs are free to expand across frontiers at will, they might do considerable national harm even while arguing that they provided the most feasible means for promoting international commerce.

RAYMOND VERNON. I am not sure that I recognize my position in your argument. That the world economy is inequitable and unstable is agreed; that any alternative arrangement of power might be better or worse is difficult to prove. It is not likely, however, that we can resolve

[25] New York: Basic Books, 1976.

the issue by moving from general propositions about international markets to specific assertions with regard to the MNEs. We might not be able to legislate a re-ordering of values and preferences in the LDCs or among MNE managers. But there are limited improvements that can be recommended. Some of them advance the cause of public sector planning, some curtail the aggressiveness of international competition, while others just leave well enough alone. We can only be pragmatic in choosing among the recommendations that are available.

For example, while consulting with LDC officials I have emphasized that they enjoyed a greater range of choice than they had imagined, both to increase the development pie and to increase their own slice of it. There is no need to turn away foreign investment or foreign technology transfers. Room can be left in negotiating with foreign entrants for the subsequent arrival of MNE competitors, or for limited import and maximum export traffic. Adequate pay scales for labor, the development of local skills, the utilization of R&D and of value-added production can also be stressed. Provision was even made in the Andean Pact for the eventual divestiture of foreign investment; this required that after a number of years elapsed, capital and plant would pass from the foreign owners to the host country. These are tough conditions to accept, but both companies and countries eventually arrived at mutually acceptable compromises.

JOSEPH MURPHY. You failed to mention two of the choices available to the LDCs when dealing with foreign investment. The first is to take it over or nationalize it. The second is to deny it entry from the outset. Considering the abuses that the poorest countries, the Group of 77, have chronicled at meetings of UNCTAD or at the Special Session of the General Assembly, these tactics and choices cannot be overlooked.

RAYMOND VERNON. Both tactics have been used with great frequency though with varying success. A large number of foreign-owned plantations and public utility companies have been nationalized in recent years, as United Fruit (now United Brands) or ITT can testify. The threat to take over or to deny entrance to foreign interests must be delicately handled, however, as future reverberations could be painful. If foreign ventures are threatened too brusquely or harshly, the queue of entering newcomers will immediately disappear; it will probably form at a nearby frontier, where controls and threats are less ominous and less risky.

In India, for example, the bureaucrats laid down such stringent requirements at the threshhold of entry that many entrants backed away. In Mexico they were more subtle. They recognized that negotiation requires biding one's time. There was a jockeying for concessions at the stage of entry and a revision at subsequent stages of development. Other LDCs have discovered that as foreign plants become deeply rooted, it is harder for them to get up and leave; it also becomes more reasonable for them to meet the escalating demands of the host nation. In short, the cost-benefit analyses of host and guest are better than either envisaged at the time of entry.

The National Interest and International Trade

ROBERT GILPIN. We have argued so far about the assumed benefits of foreign investment and trade, as well as the inability of national governments to control them. We have agreed that most of the alternatives to present arrangements are unconvincing or unattractive, and that our national planning, if it ever moves from rhetorical debate into economic reality, will stop at the water's edge. Whether or not we blame the MNE or other decision agents in the international economy, we appear to conclude that exercises in collective planning are not suitable to the arena of world trade.

A longer view of history must be taken if we are to break out of the box of this contemporary argument. For example, we can recall the perspective adopted by Lenin. He warned that the consequences of foreign investment would be experienced not only in the colonial submission of the recipients; the donor countries would react, too, largely by retarding their own technology and capital investment at home. To extend his argument, the recipient countries would be blessed with the manufacturing jobs that had been relocated from the high- to the low-wage economies; but this would leave the donors with little to do except to operate their own service industries. Is this what is happening in Britain and now in the United States?

RAYMOND VERNON. I must sharply disagree. Lenin assumed that surplus value would be deployed as capital in foreign investments. But cap-

ital is not the essential ingredient in MNE activity, especially since
much of it is raised in the host country. Critics accuse the MNE of
exploiting the capital of the host, not the home, country to enlarge its
overseas operations. Or they condemn its dispersion of jobs so that the
high-paid work remains at home and the drudgery is exported to affiliates abroad.

Neither of these accusations is correct; presumably, neither could
support an extension of Lenin's theory of imperialism. The expansion of
the U.S. automobile companies into Mexico might make the point.
Their affiliates were created in order to overcome import barriers and to
save on production costs. Once their assembly lines were working, they
had to move into more exotic activities, many of them highly paid; they
feared that otherwise they might be kicked out. This included exporting
Mexican components to their own assembly plants back in the United
States as well as conceding even greater influence to the Mexican government in the mangement decisions of the affiliate company. Instead of
exhibiting the classic responses of the exploited, the Mexican plants
began to exercise a growing role in corporate strategy.

WALTER GOLDSTEIN. Then you confirm the points that David Apter
and Robert Gilpin have tried to make. The managers of the MNE are
highly mobile in deploying capital, employment technology, or production from one country to another. If it pays General Electric to raise capital in Germany or to acquiesce in a joint venture in Mexico, the payoff
can be considerable. If necessary, G.E. or G.M. can cheaply train or
hire the workers needed to manufacture labor-intensive components to
be shipped back to the United States or to a third country. The resulting
profits are often extensive; so, too, are the enlargements of production
and marketing controls won by an aggressive MNE.

A further development along these lines is worth studying. It is con-
ceivable that the affiliates of Ford or Dow Chemicals scattered across
the nine economies of the Common Market could avoid national controls
by resorting to subtle methods of transfer pricing. By doing so they
could slip under the EEC network of monetary and currency controls, import restrictions, tariffs, and labor bargaining agreements. The MNE
does not fear that it will be kicked out, as you put it, because in most
host countries it has benefits to offer that make it too valuable to lose.
Crossing currency and political zones as it will, the MNE enjoys mo-

bility options that sovereign states cannot ignore. Too many of their export or high-growth industries are dependent on free international movements of capital and jobs.

It is difficult to accept the proposition that multinational firms will remain immune to national planning and democratic controls. Rapid growth in the capital- or technology-intensive industries of the developed world has been successfully stimulated by the entry of foreign MNEs. By contrast, the efforts of subsidized, protected, or nationalized firms have been very unimpressive. But if the benefits bestowed by international firms involve a high political cost to the nation-state, one must question whether the independent, capitalist economy will be overwhelmed by the growing forces of world trade.

RAYMOND VERNON. There are important generalizations here to be examined. First, the degree of capital or technology intensity is a function of scale in most enterprises. The most capital-intensive tend to be the big, state-owned enterprises that dominate their domestic environment. Second, foreign investment is fairly discriminating in selecting the location for new plant; it is not tied to traditional locations or urban labor centers, like local entrepreneurs. Third, the MNE cuts across numerous interests, in both the home and host societies; it throws into doubt whether there is a homogeneous "national interest" to encourage or impede its movements.

The fastest-growing sector of world trade is to be found in the manufactured exports of the LDCs, and in this growth there has been a powerful contribution from the MNE. The expansion of MNEs has been lamented by some host governments and associated with the CIA by others. But it must be noted that the number of MNEs engaged in any given product line, in any given country, has also grown. This proliferation has made the MNEs somewhat insecure, as it allows host officials to play off one MNE against the others. The relative strength in negotiating positions, therefore, has begun to switch from the mobile guest to the territorial host. It is the latter that offers the marketing or the production potential which the MNE seeks. This does not appear to herald the death of the national, capitalist economy.

I concluded my paper by noting that developed countries, such as the United States, can choose between two fundamental policies in economic planning. Either they can resort to protectionist strategies and border restrictions, or they can pursue a closer collaboration of national actions to harmonize their disparate economic interests. The first choice is ill-advised and the second has yet to yield much progress. I concluded that the need to harmonize national policies in order to maintain open borders seems fairly compelling. As nations are being pushed closer and closer together, that sort of need may prove even more powerful. The course of harmonization remains the critical issue in international commerce. It can be assisted by national planning without recourse to protectionist controls.

TECHNOLOGICAL INNOVATION FOR THE U. S. CIVILIAN ECONOMY

The Role of Government

FRANKLIN A. LONG

THE UNITED STATES, in common with virtually all of the nonsocialist nations of the world, relies principally on private industry to produce technological innovations.[1] In the past three decades, however, governmental concern for and participation in technological innovation has risen sharply. A principal component of this rise in the United States has been governmental support for military and space technology, i.e., for technologies linked directly to national security. But governments also have become more concerned with innovation for *civilian* technologies. Technological innovation is increasingly seen as a major contributor to

F. A. Long is the Henry R. Luce Professor of Science and Society and professor of chemistry at Cornell University. This paper is supported in part by grant no. SOC75-02414 to Cornell University from the National Science Foundation.

[1] The term *technological innovation* has come into general use to describe the set of activities that bring a potential new element of technology from conceptualization into actual use. Research and development (R&D) is a useful descriptive term for the earlier stages of

economic growth and as an element in international competition and international prestige.[2]

Another reason for governmental concern is that the economic growth of a nation often exhibits troublesome imbalances, i.e., there are "lagging" sectors of industrial development and of service industries, and governments may feel impelled to give special support to them. Finally, the growth of particular technologies may produce undesirable social or environmental impacts leading to the need for governmental regulation. In the United States these concerns have led to a body of government policies for civilian R&D and technological innovation and a set of programs to support the policies. These policies and programs come from a variety of agencies: (a) support agencies like the Department of Energy (DOE, formerly ERDA) and the Department of Housing and Urban Development (HUD); (b) regulatory agencies like the Environmental Protection Agency (EPA); (c) advisory and monitoring agencies like the Council of Economic Advisors and the National Science Foundation.

Specific figures on monetary costs of technological innovation are virtually impossible to obtain. However; data are available on expenditures

---

this process, but successful innovation requires an additional set of steps which are usually labeled *commercialization* and which include process design and development, manufacturing development, and market development.

It will be convenient in this discussion (although not essential) to restrict the definition of technology to "the physical means for providing objects for human sustenance and comfort," i.e., to technology as hardware, not as software. Specifically, this will exclude from the current discussion the social technologies of organization, management, welfare, and so on.

[2] Zvi Griliches, "Research Expenditures, Education, and the Aggregate Agricultural Production Function," *American Economic Review* 54, no. 6 (1964): 961–74; John U. Kendrick, *Productivity Trends in the United States* (Princeton: Princeton Univ. Press, 1961); Simon Kuznets, "Technological Innovations and Economic Growth," in *Technological Innovation: A Critical Review of Current Knowledge,* vol. 2, ed. Patrick Kelly and Melvin Kranzberg (Washington, D.C.: National Science Foundation, 1975) pp. 476–541; Edwin Mansfield, "Technological Change: Measurement, Determinants, and Diffusion," in *The Employment Impact of Technological Change,* report prepared by The National Commission on Technology and Progress (Washington, D.C., 1966); Edwin Mansfield et al., *Research and Innovation in the Modern Corporation* (New York: Norton, 1971); Richard B. Nelson, Merton J. Peck, and Edward D. Kalachek, *Technology, Economic Growth, and Public Policy* (Washington, D.C.: Brookings, 1967); Richard B. Nelson and Sidney G. Winter, "In Search of a Useful Theory of Innovation," *Research Policy,* in press; William D. Nordhaus, *Invention, Growth, and Welfare: A Theoretical Treatment of Technological Change* (Cambridge: M.I.T. Press, 1969).

for R&D, which is an important element of innovation and which can
serve as a rough measure of it.[3] Table 1 illustrates the large role of the
federal government. Over half of all R&D support comes from federal
sources. Almost two-thirds of the federal funds are for R&D in military
and space purposes. Even if one puts aside for a moment the civilian
"spin-off" from the military–space R&D, the contribution of federal
funds to civilian technology is large, roughly $6.5 billion in 1976 (com-
pared to $16.5 billion from private industry).[4]

Table 1   Estimated U.S. Expenditures for R&D for Fiscal 1976

Source of funds	Obligations, $ billions	Expenditures, $ billions	Percentage of total R&D
Private industry		16.6	43.5
Federal government		20.1	52.8
Military	10.6		
Space	2.9		
Health	2.4		
Energy	1.6		
Environment	0.98		
Science and technology base	0.86		
Other	2.0		
Universities and other not-for-profit institutions	1.4		3.7
Total		38.1	

SOURCE: Obligations (1976): National Science Foundation, "Real Increases Seen for
Federal R&D Funding of Energy, Education, Science and Defense in FY 1977," in *Science
Resources Studies Highlights,* prepared by the Government Studies Group, Division of
Science Resources Studies, NSF 76-319 (Washington, D.C., August 19, 1976); expenditures:
National Science Foundation, *National Patterns of R&D Resources, Funds, and Manpower in
the United States, 1953–1976,* NSF 76-310 (Washington, D.C.: Government Printing Office,
April 1976).

[3] A recent analysis by Stead suggests that R&D costs are typically about half of the total
costs of technological innovation. See H. G. S. Stead, "The Costs of Technological Innovation," *Research Policy* 5, no. 1 (1976): 2–9.

[4] A quite different picture emerges if one looks at a tabulation of the U.S. national R&D
effort by performer. Over two-thirds of the R&D is performed by industry; about 15 percent is performed in federal laboratories, and the remainder in universities and other not-
for-profit institutions (National Science Foundation, *National Patterns of R&D Resources,
Funds and Manpower in the United States, 1953–1976,* NSF 76–310 [Washington, D.C.:
Government Printing Office, April 1976]).

The large governmental role in R&D and in supporting technological innovation raises a number of important questions. What is the U.S. record in technological innovation? Should we be satisfied? Where in the United States does technological innovation mainly come from, i.e., which industrial groups do particularly well at innovation and which less well? Are there "problem areas," industrially speaking, where governmental assistance may be particularly needed? What have been the impacts of governmental regulations on innovation? What are the particularly useful roles of government in supporting and guiding innovation, and what changes in government direction or emphasis may be desirable?[5]

Characteristics of Innovation

Innovation comes in many forms: social and technological, product and process, civilian and military, major and minor. Even for technological innovation for the civilian economy, to which this discussion is restricted, the diversity is large. Innovation for agriculture differs considerably from that for electronics, and innovation for health differs from both. Comparable diversity exists in the industries that manufacture products for the various fields. The fact that a number of differing activities are included under the rubric of technological innovation suggests that the governmental policy and program responses may also be expected to vary; we shall shortly examine these responses.

[5] Governmental policies for R&D and technological innovation have stimulated worldwide interest and have led to a number of useful analyses and recommendations. Nelson, Peck, and Kalachek's *Technology, Economic Growth, and Public Policy,* and the "Charpie Report" from the U.S. Department of Commerce (*Technological Innovation: Its Environment and Management,* prepared by the Panel on Invention and Innovation [Washington, D.C.: Government Printing Office, 1967]) are early and influential examples. Important later analyses include those of Britain by Christopher Freeman (*The Economics of Industrial Innovation* [Baltimore: Penguin Books, 1974]) and by Keith Pavitt and W. B. Walker ("Government Policies towards Industrial Innovation: A Review," *Research Policy* 5, no. 1 [1976]: 11–97) and of the United States by Nelson and Winter ("In Search of a Useful Theory), by George Eads ("U.S. Government Support for Civilian Technology: Economic Theory Verges Political Theory," *Research Policy* 3, no. 1 [1974]: 2–16) and by Mansfield et al. (*Research and Innovation*). The extensive analysis by Robert Gilpin gives particular attention to the role of the federal government in aiding technological innovation (*Technology, Economic Growth, and International Competitiveness,* a report prepared for the Subcommittee on Economic Growth of the Joint Economic Committee, 94th Congress, 1st Session, 9 July 1975 [Washington, D.C.: Government Printing Office]).

Technological innovation and R&D directed toward it are increasingly science-based and increasingly the product of formal efforts of R&D and engineering laboratories of industry. To dramatize the growing importance of science to technology, a historian of the field, Bernard Cohen, has pointed out that as little as a hundred years ago the role of scientific ideas in technological innovation was negligible, whereas in the past fifty years science-based agriculture and health treatment, building on advances in communications, chemistry, physics, and other sciences, have changed our lives.[6] In considerable measure this increased use of scientific information has been responsible for the growth of formal R&D laboratories, staffed by trained scientists and engineers. The role of the private inventor (measured, for example, by the percentage of patents from individuals) is still important but it has declined steadily in the United States.

As both Gilpin and Nelson and Winter have emphasized, a central characteristic of innovation is that it is inherently risky and uncertain.[7] The uncertainties are many: an exciting invention may not be translatable into a viable technology; patents may not survive challenge; know-how may not be protectable; design and development costs may become excessive; market acceptance may fail to develop. A related element of risk is that in spite of patent protection and attempts at secrecy, knowledge of most innovations spreads rapidly.

The process of diffusion of knowledge and of technological innovations is itself an important characteristic of innovation. It has been extensively studied by Mansfield and others[8] and has both national and international significance. Formal modes of technology transfer, e.g., by licensing of patents and processes, constitute one aspect of diffusion. Of perhaps equal importance is diffusion by imitation, which has become so prevalent that one occasionally hears the aphorism, "It is better [i.e., less costly] to be second than first." A major factor in imitation is that the bare knowledge that a new process or product exists greatly eases the problem of an imitator. (It has been reported, for example, that

[6] "The Imagination of Nature," in *Frontiers of Knowledge in the Study of Man*, ed. Lynn White, Jr. (New York: Harper, 1956), pp. 150–65.

[7] Gilpin, *Technology, Economic Growth, and International Competitiveness*; Nelson and Winter, "In Search of a Useful Theory."

[8] *Research and Innovation*.

within a week after the announcement of transistors by Bell Laboratories, the Phillips Company in the Netherlands was able to duplicate them.)

Finally, we must note an important stepwise characteristic of the technological innovation process, especially as carried out by the larger industrial firms, which follows directly from the inherent risks of innovation. The process typically involves a stepwise sequence of project reviews, cost analyses, and accompanying decisions. Often these reviews and decisions are made at predetermined checkpoints in the developmental process (e.g., do the data from the pilot plant confirm the laboratory-bench results?). Essentially, these reviews reflect a determination to make continuing assessment of technical progress, to keep the financial risks of the project from exceeding tolerable bounds, and simultaneously to confirm that the project remains favorable from a cost-benefit point of view. In the later stages particularly, the reviews require estimates of the potential profit if the innovation is successful. Indeed, it is almost impossible to overemphasize the importance to private industry of continuous market analysis in guiding and monitoring technological innovation.[9]

In addition to the technical and market uncertainties which enter for innovations, there are uncertainties which stem from government policies and regulations. Before turning to these, however, we can appropriately look further into the sources of American innovation and the health of the enterprise.

Sources of Technological Innovation

Certain U.S. industries are far more innovative than others. Chemicals, drugs, electronics, communications, instruments, and information systems rank high among the nonmilitary fields. Most of the so-called growth industries are to be found in these fields. As would be expected, internal industry expenditures for R&D are large in these areas, both in

---

[9] When gains from innovations cannot be reckoned in dollars but only in unquantifiable benefits like "improved national security," it is far less easy to make rational decisions. If the costs of the innovation are also difficult to reckon, as might be true for many social innovations, then simple cost-benefit analysis becomes virtually impossible and decision-making becomes more involved and subjective.

absolute amounts and as a percentage of sales.[10] There seem to be no simple reasons for these particular industries to be highly innovative. A partial explanation is that they are mostly science-based fields, and the sciences on which they build are themselves expanding (e.g., chemistry and solid-state physics). But the level of innovation varies considerably among the companies in each of these industries, and indeed a selected group of industrial concerns has had the reputation of being "good at innovation" for many years. One must therefore conclude that explicit business strategies are involved in the commitment to innovation, and that perhaps sociological factors may also contribute to an ambience in which entrepreneurship flourishes.

It is sometimes argued that the slow growth of the "mature industries" (e.g., metals, food, textiles, paper, building materials) is to be explained by their low investment rate in R&D. A more plausible explanation is that these are fields of intrinsically low scientific and technological opportunity. In support of this idea, note that when new technologies and processes enter these fields it is often by "technology invasion," meaning that innovative approaches developed by the science-based industries are modified to fit some of the needs of the mature industries. An often-cited example is the chemical industry's development of synthetic polymers and synthetic fibers, which were then rapidly introduced into textile manufacturing. In other fields where innovation appears low (e.g., housing), a large contributing factor may be the fragmented structure of the industry, with no firms of sufficient size and stability to support R&D programs and to assume the substantial economic risks that innovation typically involves. One might assume that this kind of industry would respond by establishing joint industry R&D institutes or research associations. Although this does seem to be a typical response in Europe, it is not yet common in the United States.

Agriculture and health are two civilian areas in which substantial R&D programs are supported in the United States with government funds. In 1975 federal R&D expenditures for health were $2.1 billion, and state and federal funds for agriculture were about $0.75 billion. Firm data on private sector expenditures for R&D are hard to obtain but

[10] An excellent recent compendium of R&D expenditures by private industry is to be found in "Where Private Industry Puts Its Money," *Business Week*, 28 June 1976, pp. 62–84.

appear to be comparable; roughly $1.3 billion in the field of health and $0.8 billion for agriculture.[11] A principal argument for large government funding of R&D in these two areas is that the industrial structures involved—the farms for agriculture and the doctors and hospitals for medical care—represent so fragmented an industry that they cannot mount adequate programs of R&D and technology innovation. But supporting industries have developed within related fields of the private sector (e.g., the chemical industry), and it appears that technological innovation for the two fields occurs principally within these private sector industries. Examples are new instrumentation for doctors and hospitals, and new pesticides and herbicides for agriculture.[12] To a large degree the government-supported programs of R&D appear to be confined to basic and long-range applied research and to assistance in diffusing new technology to the fragmented industries.[13]

Motivation for Technological Innovation by the Private Sector

Increased profits are without doubt a major incentive for innovation by private industry, but other objectives, such as high rates of growth and increased market share, can also pertain. The objective of improved

[11] This estimated equality of public and private sector support for agricultural R&D is consistent with Byerly's 1968 data as tabulated by Kenneth E. Knight, George Kozmetsky, and Helen R. Baca, *Industrial Views of the Role of the Federal Government in Industrial Innovation* (Austin: Univ. of Texas Graduate School of Business, 1976), p. 104.

[12] A medical doctor commented recently that a dramatic illustration of the role of technology in health services is the office of a modern dentist, where one finds remarkable new techniques and materials for the care of teeth and for the comfort of the patient. Apparently these technological innovations have come almost without exception from the dental industry, responding to market opportunities.

[13] Limiting this discussion to innovations in physical technology, i.e., to hardware, probably gives a misleading picture of the importance of basic science to advances in health care. A recent analysis of major advances in the treatment of cardiovascular and pulmonary diseases suggests that most of the "top clinical advances" in this field would probably not fall within the category of *technology* since they mostly are medical and surgical procedures for treatment (Julius H. Comroe, Jr., and Robert D. Dripps, "Scientific Basis for the Support of Biomedical Science," *Science* 192 [1976]: 105–11). The detailed analysis of the origin of these major advances shows that the topics of 62 percent of the key articles on them can be categorized as basic research. Viewed in this light, the current federal programs of support for basic and long-range applied R&D may well be responding to the most important needs for innovation in the field of health care.

service often impels regulated industries to technological innovation. Companies within a given industry differ widely in their level of R&D expenditures. Some firms appear to stress short-term profitability; others take a longer view. Observers of industry will easily give examples of growth companies, conservative firms, stodgy firms. However, as Pavitt and Walker note,[14] one looks in vain for explicit analyses of why firms do or do not innovate. Analysis is particularly difficult for large firms, which typically have available a variety of strategic choices in planning for profits and for growth. In contrast, many small firms in high-technology fields are launched with the single strategy of innovation, usually building on the new ideas of their founders. But even for these, there is not much understanding of the specific pros and cons which enter into a decision to start a new business based on innovation. In sum, innovation remains a rather mysterious process, in spite of the attention and concern it has aroused. This lack of detailed understanding greatly complicates governmental attempts to foster innovation and may help explain the frequent failures of well-intentioned governmental support programs.

Ironically, it is much easier to identify disincentives to private sector innovation. At best, technological innovation is a risky business, and it follows that any new or threatened uncertainties (beyond those inherent in the new technology itself) will discourage innovation. Typical examples are uncertainties in predictions of market growth, costs of labor or capital, new or threatened regulations, or the responses of competitors. But, with the exception of the field of regulations, governmental initiatives probably cannot do much to modify these potential disincentives.

The State of Health of U.S. Technological Innovation

American expenditures for R&D, in constant dollars, have held roughly level for the past decade; this situation contrasts sharply with the preceding decade, when real growth in R&D expenditures averaged 7 percent per year for both industry and the federal government. As a

[14] "Government Policies towards Industrial Innovation."

percentage of GNP, the high mark for R&D expenditures was 3.0 percent in 1964, declining to 2.2 percent in 1976. During the last decade real R&D expenditures by industry have risen slowly at an average rate of about 2 percent per year. Federal R&D expenditures, by contrast, have declined in constant dollars by about 2 percent per year during the decade. Military R&D, as a fraction of total federal R&D expenditure, held level during the decade at about 55 percent, but declined slightly in real terms; R&D for space declined considerably in fractional terms from 24 percent of federal R&D expenditures in 1969 to 13 percent in 1976. Only in the field of energy have federal R&D expenditures moved substantially upward, from 2 percent of the federal total in 1969 to 8 percent in 1976. Owing mainly to this last item, federal obligations for R&D for civilian technology have increased moderately over the past decade in constant 1972 dollars, from $4.1 billion in 1969 to 6.1 billion in 1976, or about 5 percent per year (see table 2).[15] At best, the 1967–1976 decade experienced modest growth in civilian-oriented R&D. Relative to the 1957–1966 decade, the growth rate is lower by a factor of about two to three.

Given this recent slowdown in growth rate for R&D, it is important to ask how well the United States has been doing in technological innovation. On the basis of evidence summarized in the NSF report *Science Indicators—1974*,[16] the answer is, reasonably well (for further details, see figures 1–4). From the report one can conclude the following:

[15] In terms of tables 1 and 2, the category of *civilian technology* includes all of the federal R&D expenditures except military and space. A case can be made for including space R&D expenditures as civilian, and analysts occasionally do so (Pavitt and Walker, ibid.). My reasons for coupling military and space R&D and excluding them for the civilian category are two: the technological characteristics of military and space R&D are very similar and the program overlap is substantial; R&D in both areas is almost fully supported by the government and is in the main defended by similar arguments: national security and national prestige. It can, however, be plausibly argued that space R&D is becoming increasingly oriented toward civilian needs so that soon a more detailed subdivision may be required.

Expenditures by the third and smallest R&D support group of table 1, "Universities and other not-for-profit institutions," have also grown in real terms during the past decade. In 1972 dollars, the figures are $0.82 billion in 1967 and $1.05 billion in 1976. This indicates a real growth rate of about 2.5 percent per year.

[16] Prepared by the National Science Board (Washington, D.C.: Government Printing Office, December 1975).

Table 2 Estimated Federal R&D Obligations, 1976, Compared with 1969

Function	1976, $ millions	1976, percent of total	Obligations ratio in constant dollars, 1976 to 1969 [a]
Military and space			
National defense	10,641	49.2	0.83
Space	2,879	13.3	0.50
Subtotal	13,520	62.5	0.73
Other (civilian)			
Health	2,368	10.9	1.36
Energy development and conservation	1,632	7.5	3.23
Science and technology base	857	4.0	1.08
Environment	975	4.5	2.01
Transportation and communications	711	3.3	1.01
Natural resources	504	2.3	1.63
Food, fiber, other agricultural products	402	1.9	1.16
Education	188	0.87	0.79
Income security and social service	154	0.71	1.03
Community development, housing and public services	137	0.63	1.81
Economic growth and productivity	79	0.37	0.92
Crime prevention and control	63	0.29	8.2
International cooperation and development	34	0.16	0.82
Subtotal	8,104	37.5	1.48
Total	21,625		0.90

SOURCE: The same as for table 1, obligations.
[a]Calculated from data of NSF 76-319, using NSF deflators. Deflator ratio for 1976 and 1969 is 1.54.

1. The United States remains preeminent in the world in production of basic scientific knowledge and very strong in applied scientific research.
2. United States technical manpower for R&D is large in both absolute and comparative terms (figure 1). The percentages and numbers for R&D personnel in the USSR are considerably larger than for the United States, but there are strong doubts whether the definition of a professional is the same in the two countries.
3. The United States "patent balance" remains strongly favorable (figure 2). The positive U.S. balance has been declining in recent years, however, and one may reasonably wonder whether the balance will be positive at the end of another decade or two.
4. The United States has a strongly positive balance of payments from sale of technical know-how, i.e., licenses, patents, etc. (figure 3). This balance has risen steadily over the period 1960–1974.
5. The United States has a large favorable balance of trade in commodities produced by R&D-intensive industries (figure 4). Overall this favorable balance has increased through the years, but it has been modestly unfavorable in relation to one important country, Japan.
6. Spending on R&D by U.S. industry is large in absolute numbers and as a percentage of sales.

Despite this favorable assessment, there are numerous areas of concern. Retrospective analyses like those of *Science Indicators* are unreliable for predicting the future. More specifically, many have argued that the favorable current situation reflects the emphasis during the 1960s on R&D and innovation, and that the slowdown in R&D efforts during the last ten years bodes ill for the future. Another concern is that funds for basic and applied research, measured in constant dollars, have not increased significantly in a decade. In several areas of importance to the quality of life, e.g., housing and transportation, R&D has been and remains small. Finally, a major new need has arisen for increased R&D—the need to develop alternate energy sources to replace declining reserves of oil and gas.

(Number per 10,000 population)

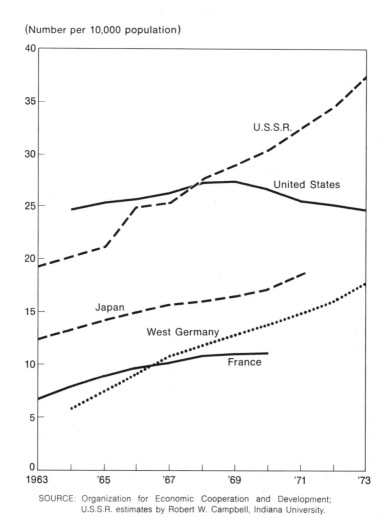

SOURCE: Organization for Economic Cooperation and Development;
U.S.S.R. estimates by Robert W. Campbell, Indiana University.

Figure 1

**Scientists and engineers engaged in R&D per 10,000 population,
by country, 1963–1973. Includes all scientists and engineers
(full-time equivalent basis). Data for Great Britain are not available.**

**Note: figures 1–4 are redrawn from <u>Science Indicators–1974</u>,
prepared by the National Science Board, National Science
Foundation (Washington, D.C.: Government Printing Office,
December 1975).**

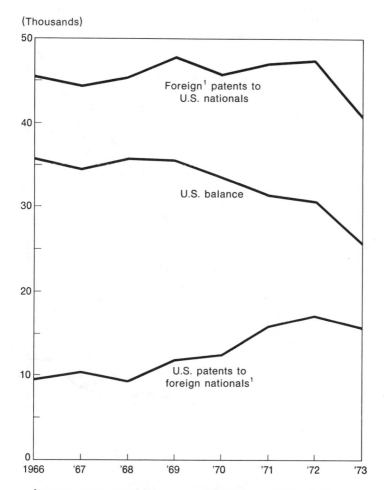

(Thousands)

Foreign[1] patents to
U.S. nationals

U.S. balance

U.S. patents to
foreign nationals[1]

[1]Including Canada, West Germany, Japan, United Kingdom, U.S.S.R., Belgium,
Denmark, Ireland, Luxembourg, and the Netherlands.
SOURCE: World Intellectual Property Organization.

Figure 2

**Patents granted to U.S. nationals by foreign countries and to
foreign nationals by the United States, 1966–1973.**

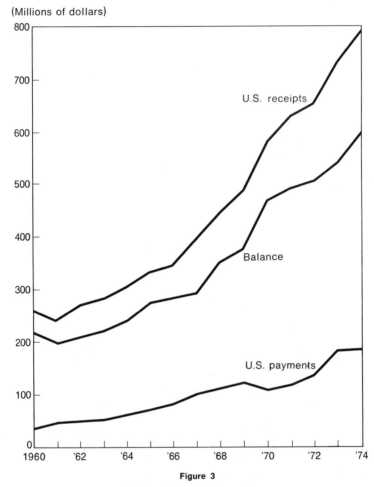

(Millions of dollars)

Figure 3

United States receipts and payments for patents, manufacturing rights, licenses, etc., 1960–1974.

The Role of Government in Technological Innovation

Governments affect programs of technological innovation for the civilian economy in three main ways:

1. Governments lend indirect support to innovation by a variety of mechanisms; for example, by supporting basic and long-range applied research.

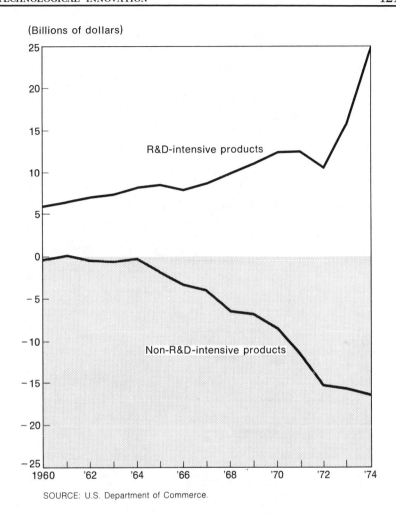

(Billions of dollars)

SOURCE: U.S. Department of Commerce.

Figure 4

United States trade balance in R&D-intensive and non-R&D-intensive manufactured products, 1960–1974.

2. Governments occasionally intervene directly in technological innovation. This is common in the military and space fields, where concern about national security is high and where the government is the major purchaser of the eventual products. Government intervention in innovation for civilian programs is not uncommon, however. National security concerns occasionally enter here also

but so do concerns about balance within the economy, e.g., about
lagging industries.
3. Governments guide and control innovations by private industry by
   means of a variety of regulations, bans, controls, and policies (implicit or explicit). Occasionally, the regulations and controls will be
   designed to assist innovation by private industry. Often, however,
   they will be established in response to national priorities other
   than innovation, e.g., environmental protection.

Enhanced economic growth, which is given high priority in most nations, is commonly cited as the chief reason for governmental support
for technological innovation. Other national priorities will occasionally
conflict directly with the goal of economic growth, however, and regulations which stem from these priorities may inhibit or even prevent some
industry programs of technological innovation (while simultaneously encouraging others). Since the United States now has one of the highest
per capita GNPs of the world, it should not be surprising that priorities
other than growth, priorities of the kind that can be labeled "quality of
life," have become more important in recent years and have in turn influenced the regulatory atmosphere. Industry cannot, of course, contest
the right of government to establish regulations which restrict or re-
direct some of its programs. It can, however, reasonably expect that the
regulations will be effective in accomplishing their stated purposes, and
it can also expect that the regulations will be developed and imposed in
ways that do not unnecessarily, or perhaps inadvertently, inhibit programs of innovation or growth which otherwise would be in the national
interest.

In practice, regulations are probably the most troubling and irritating
of the governmental impacts on innovation; hence, we discuss them
first.

The Impact of Government Regulations, Controls, Tax Policies

Regulations and controls take many forms: environmental regulations
and requirements for environmental impact statements, price controls,
export controls, regulations and test protocols for toxicity and car-
cinogenicity, safety regulations. They are in effect the action arm for

governmental policies and represent a principal mechanism by which a government guides industry and other groups in directions that presumably reflect the national interest. The impact of U.S. federal regulatory agencies on industry is large and growing. Table 3 lists some of the major agencies and illustrates the fact that the regulatory approach varies considerably among them.

Regulations are sometimes explicitly designed to aid technological innovation; import controls and tariffs, for example, have been designed to assist infant industries. Often, regulations are designed, implicitly or explicitly, to bring about changes in the direction of innovation. For example, the imposition of automotive emission controls has accelerated innovation in automotive engines. The major complaints from industry concerning regulations tend, therefore, not to be about the national goals for which they have been developed, but rather about their short-term direct and indirect impacts on industrial activities.

From the standpoint of technological innovation, the major complaint is that regulations frequently introduce large delays and uncertainties in the already risky development of new technologies. By far the most vigorous reaction to environmental regulations (the need for which is quite

Table 3   Federal Agencies' Regulatory Influence on Industry

Selected regulatory agencies	Specific industry	Business function	All firms
Federal Drug Administration	X		
Federal Aviation Agency	X		
Federal Energy Agency	X		X
Federal Power Commission	X		X
Environmental Protection Agency		X	X
Occupational Safety & Health Administration		X	X
Equal Employment Opportunity Commission		X	X
Interstate Commerce Commission	X		X
Civil Aeronautics Board	X		X
Federal Communications Commission	X		X
Federal Trade Commission			X
Nuclear Regulatory Commission	X		

SOURCE: Kenneth E. Knight, George Kozmetsky, and Helen R. Baca, *Industrial Views of the Role of the Federal Government in Industrial Innovation* (Austin: Univ. of Texas Graduate School of Business, 1976).

generally accepted) is that, as promulgated and as argued out in courts, they have produced very substantial delays and uncertainties.[17]

A related impact of regulations is that they often necessitate a reorientation of R&D efforts toward defensive research, i.e., research to modify processes or products to permit them to satisfy new regulations. Industry argues that this kind of R&D competes with and distracts from the R&D directed toward innovations of the sort that have led to industrial growth and profitability.[18]

A broad and important thrust of regulation and control by the U.S. government appears in its investment policies, tax policies, and import-export controls. Many of the current government regulations have been instituted to aid industry and support economic growth. Investment tax credits have without doubt been helpful. The expensing of R&D expenditures for tax purposes has probably had a favorable effect, as have federal regulations that prohibit foreign dumping of products into the U.S. market. What is not so clear is whether the total impact of these various regulations has substantially enhanced the level of technological innovation. Even less clear, particularly in view of our ignorance of why industries innovate, is whether modifications in these and related regulations would be additionally helpful.

It is occasionally charged that tax policies have inhibited technological innovation, particularly in small, high-technology business ventures. It has been argued that some of the efforts to close tax loopholes have made it more difficult for such small businesses to obtain venture capital. Similarly, it appears that some of the benefits which are useful to es-

[17] Interestingly, once regulations are well established and accepted, they can also *reduce* uncertainty since they provide ground rules which apply equally to all regions and to all the firms of an industry. A less happy way in which uncertainty is occasionally reduced is when "industry representatives" become a dominant voice in a regulatory agency, leading to the phenomenon which has been characterized as "regulation by the regulated."

[18] A recent industrial analysis is contained in a survey of 37 companies doing pesticide research (National Agricultural Chemicals Association, *1975 Industry Profile Study* [Washington, D.C., 1976]). The data led the Association to conclude that about 35 percent of the companies' research expenditures in 1975 were responding to EPA requirements, safety regulations, and so on, leaving only 65 percent for the discovery, development, and registration of new products. The report also states that in spite of these defensive expenditures, the time involved in making a newly discovered pesticide available to growers has lengthened to about eight years. The sales figures of the report make it clear, however, that despite increased regulation the industry has experienced substantial growth.

tablished companies (e.g., the opportunity to deduct R&D expenses and depreciation from income) are not especially helpful to small companies, most of which have no taxable income in their early stages. Again, the argument from industry is not that the government should not modify tax laws to prevent tax loopholes nor that it should not establish rules for treating R&D costs, depreciation, and capital gains. The argument is rather that, in making these rules, not enough attention is paid to their impact on technological innovation by industries large and small.

Government Programs of Indirect Support for R&D for Civilian Technological Innovation

The large federal R&D expenditures for civilian technology (see tables 1 and 2) constitute explicit support for innovation. In discussing them it is useful, if occasionally somewhat arbitrary, to divide the expenditures into *indirect support* and *direct intervention*, where the latter refers to government expenditures giving direct assistance to specific programs of technological innovation.

One of the most important indirect support programs is the large federal expenditure on basic research and long-range applied research in the natural and social sciences. The argument for government support in these areas is that the impact of basic and long-range applied (or pioneering) research is so wide-ranging and so uncertain in terms of time and place (i.e., yielding external rather than internal benefits) that industrial firms have little incentive to invest in such research. At the same time, the evidence is strong that over time this research makes substantial contributions to technological innovation. Since almost all developed nations provide extensive governmental support for basic and pioneering research, it appears that this argument is widely accepted. In the United States, nonfederal support in these research areas is also considerable. Universities and other not-for-profit institutions contribute importantly to basic research. The industrial contribution to basic research is modest, but to applied research it is sizable.[19]

As noted earlier, total expenditures for basic and applied research

[19] National Science Foundation, *National Patterns of R&D Resources, Funds and Manpower.*

have grown only slightly in constant dollars over the past decade. Federal support for basic research has decreased slightly; that for applied research is up slightly. Nonfederal funds have apparently grown at a slightly higher rate than federal expenditures.[20] The fact that expenditures in these areas have grown very little in real terms for a decade suggests that this may be a problem area for the United States.

A second area of indirect governmental support to R&D and to technological development in general is contributions to the advanced education of scientists, engineers, and other professionals. This translates into support of graduate education in the relevant scientific and professional disciplines in the universities. Roughly two-thirds of the advanced degrees in the United States are awarded by state universities, so expenditures by state governments are a major component of this support. Federal contributions, however, which come to both state and private universities by way of grants for research, equipment, traineeships, and postdoctoral support, are large and important. In constant dollars, federal support for advanced education has decreased substantially over the last decade.[21] One might assume that, over the long term, the net rate of growth in numbers of these professionals should not be less than the growth in the GNP, and that federal support should rise at least proportionately. But, because numbers of these students have been high in recent years and because of a markedly decreased demand for people with advanced training in one important field of work (teaching in colleges and universities), it appears that the supply of scientists and engineers with doctorates will exceed demand for at least the next decade.[22] This raises questions about the desired character of governmental sup-

[20] A recent critique of the NSF methodology as used in *Science Indicators—1974* raises doubt about the utility of the constant-dollar approach for measuring trends in research support and also argues that "funds to universities" may be a more useful measure of supportive long-range R&D than the current NSF categories of basic and applied research (L. T. Crane, *"Science Indicators—1974" and Basic Research: A Partial Analysis* [U.S. Library of Congress, 1976]). The use of this alternate criterion does not change the trends described.

[21] National Science Foundation, *Federal Support to Universities, Colleges, and Selected Nonprofit Institutions, Fiscal Year 1974,* Surveys of Science Resources Series, NSF 76–305 (Washington, D.C.: Government Printing Office, January 1976).

[22] National Science Foundation, *Projections of Science and Engineering Doctorate Supply Utilization, 1980 and 1985,* NSF 75–301 (Washington, D.C.: Government Printing Office, February 1975).

port for advanced training, one implication being that increased emphasis should go to higher quality of education, and perhaps to more programs of continuing education, rather than to larger numbers of entrants.

Two small but interesting programs providing explicit incentives for technological innovation were established by federal agencies during the early 1970s, when there was substantial concern about the adequacy of innovation in the United States. One of these is within NSF: Applied Science and Research Applications (ASRA, formerly RANN). Funding for this program has fluctuated considerably but has been on the order of $60 million per year. Essentially, this is a program of applied research with a particular focus on ultimate use of the results. Not surprisingly, a substantial number of ASRA projects are carried out solely by industry or jointly by industry and university groups. A somewhat different kind of federal incentive program is the Experimental Technology Incentives Program (ETIP) of the National Bureau of Standards. This is a modestly funded but apparently useful effort to experiment on a variety of activities within the federal agencies which can serve as indirect devices to encourage innovation in industry. Typical areas of experimentation are modifications of government procurement policy and use of performance specifications by governmental agencies. Both ETIP and ASRA have existed for too short a time to permit a confident evaluation of their impact.

Health and agriculture were cited earlier as fields where governmental expenditures for R&D are large but where the major fraction of the governmental support is complementary rather than directly supportive, i.e., that private industry is mainly responsible for extending the commercial uses of the new technologies in both fields. I do not wish to minimize the importance of the government's contribution, however, since it is responsible for most of the needed basic and applied research and also contributes largely to the diffusion of new technologies and techniques.

This analysis of indirect government support programs for technological innovation omits one area to which great significance has sometimes been attached, that of civilian spin-off from military and space R&D programs. A partial excuse for the omission is that the subject of spin-off is large and complex, and its analysis is complicated by the fact that most

R&D for military technology is classified. Nevertheless, the spin-off phenomenon is real and significant. Even if only 10 percent of military and space R&D is relevant to innovation for the civilian technologies (a reasonable estimate), the magnitude of federal support programs for military and space R&D, currently approaching $15 billion per year, means that spin-off might contribute the equivalent of $1.5 billion for civilian R&D, i.e., a 20 percent addition to direct federal expenditures. Two recent studies sponsored by the National Aeronautics and Space Administration give examples and cost-benefit analyses of spin-off from NASA programs and conclude that the benefit is substantial.[23]

Direct Governmental Intervention in Technological Innovation

Direct, supplemental programs of government support for technological innovation have become commonplace even in those developed nations that rely mainly on private industry for innovation. The arguments for direct support are various, but usually come down to a belief that market forces, even when assisted by indirect government support, cannot be depended on to produce innovations of the character and timeliness that government agencies believe are needed. The largest field for direct government support is military and space technology, but this is a special situation since there is no conventional market for the ultimate products, in that the government is the only purchaser.[24] But even for civilian technology, direct government intervention is frequent.

The recent analysis by Pavitt and Walker[25] concluded that the large European nations have intervened mostly in such high-technology fields as nuclear power, aircraft, and computers. In some instances (e.g., nuclear power), the argument for government intervention has been that

[23] Omission in our calculations of federal expenditures for civilian technological innovation of any contributions from spin-off is crudely justified by the fact that they are offset by about the same amount of R&D expenditures by industry (all of which we have labeled "civilian") on military and space projects. For further details see *Science* 193, no. 4 (1976).

[24] The rapidly rising international trade in armaments is an apparent exception to this last statement. Here also, however, purchasers must gain approval from the U.S. Department of Defense for sales by U.S. corporations; in addition there are often U.S. congressional loans or grants to the foreign purchasers. Hence, there is not a conventional market.

[25] "Government Policies towards Industrial Innovation."

the local industries could not afford the magnitude of financial risk involved in innovation. In other cases the strength of the foreign competition (e.g., IBM for computers) was considered so formidable that the risks of innovation by private enterprise were intolerably large. In almost all cases an additional and general argument for intervention was that the nation needed to be independent of foreign suppliers.

In the United States the principal civilian field for direct government support of innovation has been in technologies for nuclear power. A partial explanation is that the civilian programs grew out of military programs for nuclear power plants and uranium enrichment. The United States has, however, contemplated supplemental support in other areas (for example, supersonic aircraft and electrically powered automobiles) and it is now actively considering intervention in various nonnuclear energy programs.

The usefulness of direct government support of innovation is controversial. Analyses by Gilpin, Pavitt and Walker, Freeman, and others of efforts by European governments indicate that direct government intervention, especially in fields where market forces play a large role and where the industries are reasonably effective, is not usually successful and should normally be avoided. There are, however, areas of exception. We have already noted the role of government in health and agriculture. Governments also often feel impelled to intervene in "lagging industries," whether the lag is a consequence of genuine internal problems (e.g., a fragmented industry) or a normal result of international market activities. "National security" is almost invariably invoked when government interventions are major.[26]

Many recent analyses of the state of technological innovation in the United States have concluded that the levels of R&D and technological innovation are generally inadequate and that it behooves the government to "do something." A good recent example is the *Review of the Annual Report on Federal Research and Development Program: Fiscal Year 1976,* from the Congressional Committee on Science and Technol-

[26] An area in which government intervention is almost unavoidable is that of *social technologies.* Usual areas of concern are public health, welfare programs, community development, and education. Typically in these fields, market forces are absent or negligible. And in contrast to the situation for technological innovation, most of these fields are ones in which governments have assumed direct responsibility for progress.

ogy. The review was accomplished under Congressman Ray Thornton, chairman of the Subcommittee on Domestic and International Scientific Planning and Analysis, and solicited the views of a number of experts in and out of government. Although the report is restrained in its recommendations, focusing mostly on complementary programs for the federal government, its "generally gloomy outlook for the national R&D picture" is a point of view which can lead as easily to questionable programs of direct intervention as to useful complementary ones.[27]

New Directions for Government Programs of Support and Guidance for Technological Innovation

The preceding sections have discussed various ways in which federal policies and expenditures have direct or indirect impacts on U.S. programs of technological innovation for the civilian sector of the economy. Overall, the federal impact is large. This, and the general and particular concerns about the health of U.S. technology, make it important to ensure that the relevant federal policies and programs are effective and are directed toward the most significant problems. Because the U.S. record of technological development is good, and because many of the present governmental policies and programs have been tested and adjusted to over periods of many years, it would almost surely be a mistake to call for major reorientation of governmental efforts. Even so, a few new programs seem needed, and changes in magnitude and emphasis would be

[27] The most interesting and important of the current federal programs for support of technology innovation are those of the Department of Energy in the fields of energy conservation, energy supply, and alternate energy sources. The plans call for extensive direct support of innovation programs with the expectation, however, that private industry will eventually commercialize the results (U.S. Energy Research and Development Administration, *A National Plan for Energy Research, Development, and Demonstration: Creating Energy Choices for the Future*, vol. 1, ERDA 76-1 [Washington, D.C.: Government Printing Office, 1976]). This implies the need to develop effective industry-government collaboration on a scale and of a variety which have so far been unusual in the U.S. civilian economy. Given the somewhat disappointing record of government's indirect support for technological innovation, there is reason for skepticism about some of DOE's efforts. Since the DOE program raises a number of other important problems, such as the proper balance between nuclear and nonnuclear energy programs and the proper role of the DOE-supported laboratories, a continuing critical analysis of the DOE efforts seems essential.

helpful in a number of current areas of support and regulation. Comments follow in a few possibilities.

1. *Improved federal support of basic and long-range applied research.* Federal support is of central importance in basic and long-range applied research. Most of the important programs in these areas are carried out in universities and federally supported laboratories; federal support is necessary for all of them. It is not easy to decide on the desired national level of support for research. The fact that federal support has declined over the last decade strongly suggests, however, that research needs examination and probably increased support. A plausible long-term goal is for federal support of basic and long-range applied research to grow at a rate at least equal to the growth of the GNP.

Of equal importance to decisions on growth rates is a consideration of the specific expenditures for basic and long-range applied research. One question is, Who is to carry out the research, i.e., which components are best done in universities and which by federal laboratories or other groups? A second is, What are the high-priority areas, especially for applied research? If, as seems desirable, most of the federal support for applied research comes from the mission-oriented federal agencies, most of the decisions on levels and types of research will be made by interested "user" groups. Some consideration of the overall U.S. effort will surely be needed, however, and the reestablished Office of the President's Science Advisor, possibly working with the Domestic Council, may be the place to evaluate the national effort.

2. *An improved federally supported data-collecting and reporting system.* The analyses and reports produced by the Division of Science Resources Studies of the NSF have become invaluable in understanding U.S. programs of research and development.[28] They should certainly be continued. So too should the concern for technological innovation on the part of NSF or the Department of Commerce. They should institute additional data collection and analyses to focus on innovation and the ef-

---

[28] See, for example *An Analysis of Federal R&D Funding by Function, Fiscal Years 1969–1976,* Surveys of Science Resources Series, NSF 75-330 (Washington, D.C.: Government Printing Office, August 1975) and *Federal Funds for Research, Development, and Other Scientific Activities, Fiscal Years 1974, 1975, and 1976,* vol. 24, Surveys of Science Resources Series, NSF 75-334 (Washington, D.C.: Government Printing Office, December 1975).

forts of the private sector. A major omission in the current analyses is a breakdown by function of industrially funded programs of research and development. It would be interesting, for example, to know the total U.S. expenditure for R&D in agriculture and the separate contributions from government, from industry, and from private sources. It would also be useful to have R&D expenditures by industry tabulated annually by field of endeavor and by firm, as in the *Business Week* article cited. Finally, it will be important to have comparative analyses of the R&D expenditures and support procedures for the major developed nations of the world, in particular the OECD nations, including Japan.

3. *Development and support of new intra-industry institutions for applied research and demonstration.* A number of characteristics are desirable for intra-industry research programs. In contrast to individual firms, an establishment which represents an entire industry can appropriately undertake relatively long-range basic and applied research for the benefit of all. Institutions of this sort can also enter with relative ease into collaborative programs with universities, where the focus is on relatively long-range research, and also with government, where the focus may be on shorter-range programs of development and demonstration. A good example of this kind of laboratory is the Electric Power Research Institute (EPRI). Forming a consortium of this sort is apparently simpler for regulated industries; however, a recent analysis by the Department of Commerce suggests that under appropriate arrangements other industrial groups can probably safely establish such intra-industry research associations without fear of antitrust suits. A final comment is that the European nations seem to have gone farther along these lines that has the United States, so careful studies of the characteristics and effectiveness of European research associations would be useful.

4. *More effective use of federal laboratories for technological innovation.* The United States is committed to support an extensive array of federal laboratories for research and development. Although a number of these are directly focused on military and space technology, the majority are concerned with long-range research relevant to the civilian technology. As one notable example, the laboratories which report to DOE have annual budgets of over $1 billion and employ more than

35,000 workers. There are two major requirements, in addition to the basic needs of high-quality staff and equipment, for these federally supported laboratories to be maximally effective. The first is to ensure that, from a program standpoint, the laboratories are oriented toward problems of national significance. The second requirement is to ensure that the laboratories establish and maintain good working linkages with the university research groups on the one hand and private industry on the other.

5. *A continuing assessment of government regulations and procedures as they affect technological innovation.* There is ample evidence that a number of government policies and regulations inhibit technological innovation by industry (others,, not surprisingly, support such innovation). It is reasonable to expect the government to design its policies and regulations so as not to inhibit innovation unnecessarily or inadvertently. Regulations do not always work out as intended, and the situations for which regulations or policies may have been instituted do change. For both of these reasons, it seems important to have a continuing evaluation of the effect of government policies and regulations on innovation. When it comes to existing regulations, maybe all one can expect is separate evaluations by government groups and by industry. One can urge, however that the development of new policies and regulations will improve the interaction between government and industry; the general goal is to achieve the regulations which the government believes are necessary but to do so in ways that minimize undesirable impacts on industry.[29]

6. *Government restraint in direct intervention in programs of technological innovation.* The usual argument for direct government intervention into innovation is that the normal market forces have failed; the frequent explanation of the presumed failure is that private industry un-

---

[29] A good example of interactive development of regulations is the recently signed Toxic Substances Act, which is designed to minimize the likelihood that toxic new chemicals will be commercialized. The bill for this purpose was initially drafted by EPA but has been greatly modified by Congress as a result of extended interactions between EPA, the chemical industry, and the congressional committees involved. The result appears to be a bill that both satisfies EPA that the regulations involved and test procedures prescribed are adequate and satisfies industry that the procedures are not unnecessarily onerous or expensive.

derinvests in R&D because of unfavorable externalities. As Eads has
pointed out in his cogent analysis,[30] the actual situation is usually much
more complex than these arguments imply; furthermore, the difficulties
often vary widely from industry to industry. At the minimum, these dis-
crepancies suggest a need for detailed analyses of specific problem areas
before a government agency decides to intervene. Even when the analyses strongly suggest that R&D in a particular field is inadequate, it does
not follow that direct governmental support of innovation is the best
response. Additional government support of long-range basic and applied research, or provision of indirect financial incentives, or modifica-
tion of regulations to remove disincentives may be more effective
measures.

There is a real and serious dilemma for all government programs of
support for innovation: how to ensure, in the absence of the discipline of
financial profit and loss, that the programs are cost-effective in their own
terms and yet are broadly in the national interest. A problem of comparable seriousness for the government is how to ensure that programs
which have become irrelevant or counterproductive do not continue.
The key to both situations can be stated simply: step-by-step approaches
and continuing evaluation of effectiveness. However, to carry these out
effectively in a complex political and economic atmosphere is anything
but easy.

[30] "U.S. Government Support for Civilian Technology."

Discussion

Estimating the Costs and Benefits of R&D

MURRAY WEIDENBAUM. Although Franklin Long has noted that the data were incomplete, they nevertheless show that extensive changes in the federal funding of R&D have taken place in the past three decades. In retrospect we can see that many of the changes were transitory or inadvertent. For a start, most of the federal support came in NASA or military-purpose categories; the support varied over the years with the changing priorities of space or defense expenditures and with the changing tempo of the Cold War. Now a new priority in federal R&D expenditures has become extremely important. The President and the Congress, in providing a large budget for energy research, have emphasized the expansion of energy technologies as a national goal. The expansion is sure to continue over future years. Whether energy research will deflect resources from expensive military programs has yet to be determined.

ELI GINZBERG. The high R&D content of military or energy funding must be distinguished from the softer efforts in social or biomedical research. When spending on Medicaid and Medicare increased after 1965, biomedical funding failed to grow comparably. President Johnson, among others, insisted that the doctors had failed to produce the breakthrough results that had been promised after twenty years of intensive support. His disenchantment was reflected in the subsequent decline of R&D allocations. A similar note of discouragement appeared in the construction industry. Congress moved against the research funding for low-cost housing, and the decision has yet to be reversed. The inference can be drawn that R&D priorities reflect political enthusiasms or emergency requirements, no matter how illusory these might be.

FRANKLIN LONG. Widespread objections have been registered against a potentially important proposal: that we should monitor the aggregate input and output of industrial R&D budgets to determine whether they are socially advisable. If we assume that monitoring procedures will stiffen regulatory controls and planning formulae, the objections will be of considerable concern. But if that assumption is not valid, a stronger case can be made for a national audit, somewhat akin to the publications of the National Science Foundation. Its annual *Science Indicators* are extremely useful; they have improved the evaluation of federal programs and of the $16.6 billion spent on R&D by private industry. No one knows how the latter sum is spent, except in broad aggregate categories, or what it produces. The private outlay is equal to 43.5 percent of our national R&D expenditures of $38 billion. We need to track down, rather than to monitor, what financial and scientific outlays are included in these huge amounts.

ELI GINZBERG. I see nothing wrong in keeping track of private funding. We still do not know how to assess the quality of industrial research or the technological advances financed by GE, IBM, or DuPont. It is time to ask whether their historical record over the last twenty years has been productive. Nor is it an invasion of privacy to determine the relationship between the dollars invested and their research output. These are matters important to public policy.

FRANKLIN LONG. Although I agree, I repeat that it is difficult to derive reliable correlations or even to explain the shifting priorities of R&D. It is obvious that criticism intensifies when any major change in allocations is proposed or when the incremental growth of R&D exceeds the growth of GNP. Planning decisions are questioned, too, when an agency like DOE receives a sizable infusion of research funding or when there is a switch in mission—to solar, geothermal, or fast-breeder programs. That the nation is now obsessed with the energy issue is readily apparent. But that we will profit from crash funding programs is very doubtful.

I must also concur with Eli Ginzberg on industrial technology. Private firms know how much to pay for R&D but they do not always know what to expect from it; their gross accounting methods offer the public sector no useful guidance. Admittedly, profit-and-loss accounts provide concrete parameters for firms, like IBM or the drug companies, that spend 7 percent of their turnover on R&D. But their managers tend to be as subjective in allocating advertising outlays or promotional budgets as they are in funding new technology. Both measurements are geared to subjective projections of their product markets.

JAMES RYAN. That is an important point. AT&T spends almost $1 billion a year on R&D but we do not know until years later whether we chose the right allocations or not. It is like putting money in the collection plate on Sunday morning; you do not discover what you bought for yourself until it is too late to change your mind.

AT&T is now investing in fiber optics and light-wave transmission processes. The motives are largely economic. Urban conduits are already too jammed to allow us to increase our communications lines in metropolitan areas, and the cost of wiring new conduits is astronomical. It is assumed that optics research will enlarge the capacity of traffic and reduce capital costs. We can not afford the cost overrun of the C-5^A that Lockheed presented to the Defense Department, but neither can we afford to delay our R&D planning. The accelerating growth rates in telecommunications require an ever greater lead-time for planning; moreover, our advances in technology and services must be financed out of the profits that have to be assured in the years to come.

DEAN OSTRUM. This last point requires elaboration. Most of the work done at Bell Laboratories is "applied" in character, and a major part of it is devoted to meeting needs posed by increases in the volume of traffic. Economic feasibility studies indicate that further increases are likely but that the timing is uncertain, so the risks are great.

Bell Labs determines its research schedules by working closely with the operating companies and their engineering departments, on one side; and with our manufacturing arm, Western Electric, on the other. Decisions at the Labs are made on a case-by-case, or a year-by-year, basis in consultation with other parts of the Bell System. In this manner, fundamental research and product development can keep in step, and development priorities can be linked to projections of service requirements and market demands. In planning the research schedules we also have to consider external variables, such as future equipment needs, the rate and direction of technological change, or the time costs of expanding capacity. These are the economic and technical projections in which the private sector excels.

JOSEPH MURPHY. But surely you have omitted a critical factor: the contributions made by government in granting investment credits, tax waivers, and other legal benefits. If the government chooses, it can subsidize economic research or military technology; it can bestow favors to strengthen your competitors; or it can hand the work to AT&T. If government gave tax benefits to Disneyland for R&D, the social outcome would be strongly challenged, while the benefits distributed to gaint corporations are not. Research communities have clustered around the research parks of IBM, G.E., or Bell Labs because of the concentration in federal outlays. Research workers might have dispersed across the nation, scattering their knowledge into smaller firms and smaller colleges, if rewards had been allocated to encourage smaller communities. This switch might have retarded the advancement of sophisticated and concentrated technology; but it might also have improved the distribution of skills and intellectual attainments in our society. The social distribution of skilled work and cultural stimuli should not be ignored when we review the goals for which R&D should aim.

Measuring the Utility of R&D

ROBERT GILPIN. An evaluation of the performance of R&D in our society must be attempted even if the indicators are somewhat crude. Our national security and industrial welfare depend to a considerable degree on the productivity of research in the public and private sectors. Performance measurements of R&D may be arguable but indicators of economic growth, industrial vitality, and international standing are clearly of greater reliability; moreover, they provide some guidance to the value of the basic or the applied research that is funded at nearly $40 billion a year. We can no longer shrug aside the task of evaluating the worth of R&D by referring, as many scientists do, to the proverbial response of the man who was asked, "How's your wife?" and who replied, "Compared to what?"

Three categories of evaluation must be attempted. First, how does the present record of research and innovation compare to our performance in previous years? Second, how does it compare to the achievements of our international rivals? Third, how far does it satisfy or anticipate changing social needs?

Although there are no clear-cut replies to these three questions, they must be carefully answered. To begin with the historical record, we can compare dollar inputs in absolute sums or in relation to the rise in GNP. The expenditure curves are highly revealing but the output measurements, unfortunately, are not. We can collect crude data regarding the scientific patents that are registered, the Nobel Prizes won, or the commercial value of breakthroughs achieved in industrial or military technology. Leaving the space effort and its commercial spillover aside, the recent benchmarks on the historical record are not particularly impressive. We have not maintained the impetus of scientific expansion that was attained twenty or more years ago.

There are two categories of answers to the second question, relating to our international performance. Ray Vernon believes that we have maintained our lead over the Russians in military research, and over the Germans and Japanese in industrial technology. Other critics, including specialists in the U.S. Department of Commerce, insist that there has been a prolonged decline in American competitiveness. Serious evidence has been marshaled by both sides to support their arguments. I find parts of the evidence for either argument to be compelling; our science efforts are preeminent in most areas, but the rate of growth has not matched the accomplishments of our leading competitors.

The third evaluation provokes a host of subjective questions. How far have we moved to anticipate emerging demands or to satisfy basic social needs? How far has the national obsession with military superiority and industrial growth deflected our scientific resources? It has already been suggested that if we encourage the wrong industries we will not be able to provide useful work for 20 million more people. Our failure to fund research in biomedical, housing, and educational activities has merited considerable criticism. It has become clear that many social needs have been ignored; and so, too, has the erosion in the economic base of the nation's competitive power.

On this last score we must mention the decline in our international standing. Although we have recently retreated from the pretension to

global or imperial power, we have yet to determine what role the
United States should play in world affairs. Our retreat followed the international turmoil in Vietnam and elsewhere, and it need not necessarily be regretted. But there is no cause to resign ourselves to a
concomitant decline in the balance of payments and in our position as a
world banker.

In the postwar years we retained our economic leadership by drawing
down our gold and currency reserves; we drew down from $50 billion 25
years ago to about $10 billion at the present time. As the world's banker,
we printed a vast sum of money and forced other nations to accept it
under a system of fixed exchange rates. Today we face a less favorable
system of floating exchange rates, and we have lost some of our command over the world's reserves of natural resources. By forcing ourselves to maintain expensive garrisons in NATO and the Far East, we
have reduced our ability to pay our way on the strength of our technological leadership.

It must be questioned, therefore, whether the United States has now
entered into the same cycle of decline that marked Britain's slippage as a
world power in this century. As the pace of foreign competition intensified, we have moved toward measures of technological protectionism
to maintain our fading supremacy. It is no longer certain that we can
support a "free trade" with respect to technology and R&D. The critical
question to be faced is straightforward: Should we hold on to our own
technology or should we continue to transfer it under license and joint
venture arrangements with other countries?

WALTER GOLDSTEIN. The questions raised by Bob Gilpin go beyond
the decision of protection or free trade in the transfer of U.S. technology. There are scarce resources to be conserved in the research efforts
of the public and private sectors. Three resource factors are particularly
important.

First, in the training and employment of skilled personnel we must
determine whether the correct priorities are being pursued by graduate
schools, government research centers, and private industry. Second, in
the allocation of R&D budgets we must distinguish between commercial
or short-term needs and the larger requirements of our technologically
intensive society. I suspect we are equipped to service only the former

and that our disregard of the latter might prove to be a very costly mistake. Third, there is a vital concern for development, rather than research, that has been overlooked. It is assumed that the interplay of market forces or the demands of national security will finance future development choices, but I am not at all sure that these assumptions are still valid.

Clearly, there is a need to plan the optimum deployment and utilization of these three factors. Whether the planning should be left to entrepreneurs in the private sector or to public-agency managers remains to be determined. Advocates of corporate autonomy insist that allocations are more likely to be cost-effective if they are tied to profit considerations and a competitive market. But they forget that the most expensive R&D is financed by industries that are not competitive and that enjoy the privileges of pricing at a flexible cost plus-fixed-fee. Advocates of public planning respond that government knows more than private industry about the overall needs of R&D because it supplies the major source of funds. But they, too, overlook the fact that state-directed research is best geared to price-inelastic demand curves, as in the military or space programs, and these account for nearly 40 percent of the nation's research efforts.

It is difficult to gauge whether we are receiving the best value from our R&D budgets or whether we would do better to invest in longer-term research projects. Pleading the priority of national security will not help us deflect our energies to more constructive or neglected sectors, such as housing, new energy sources, or social improvement. Nor will we resolve this fundamental dilemma by hitching our technology funding to the vagaries of the market or to emerging probabilities of profit. Ideological interests may be served by advocating public or private sector programs, but they will not help identify the planning priorities that should be pursued.

Each of the papers presented so far has stressed the reality of cooperation and overlap between the activities of the public and the private sectors. In no activities is the collaboration more vital than in the training of personnel, the financing of research, and the subsidizing of development. We take pride in our international record of innovation, yet we do little to forge ahead in the social assessment of technology. Leaving future choices to the whims of the market or to the shifting enthusiasms of the military seems to be the worst solution to our dilemma. If we are to be a science-based society, we need to evaluate what our planning priorities should be and how social requirements can best be anticipated.

ELI GINZBERG. These are important points to follow. At different times in our history we have insisted on stabilizing the research environment, on promoting the spin-off from public or military R&D, or on optimizing the use of our resources. But we still do not know how to do all these things efficiently. Our workless physics graduates move from nuclear engineering to business administration and our most cherished technology is transferred under license to our international competitors. Worse yet, there is conspicuous waste in the large organizations that dominate the various fields of research. Whether the organizations are to be found in massive government programs or among industrial corporations that fund expensive programs and employ hundreds of skilled people, there is too much energy wasted in moving papers internally or in blocking off the innovations of smaller organizations. To cite just one example: armed with government awards and benefits, the automobile companies put vast resources into a very light technology. Their aim was not to secure the returns that Bob Gilpin and Walter Goldstein listed, but simply to protect their market position.

FRANKLIN LONG. I can only summarize by voicing my concern about our roller-coaster performance. I agree that the scale of organization has tended to vary inversely with the productivity of research. Edward Mansfield's studies reveal that maximum effectiveness per unit size is reached before the largest outfits become aware of their decline in marginal product. My example, unlike Eli Ginzberg's, is taken from the public rather than the private sector. Although the civilian spin-off from military programs might be as high as 10 percent, the defense and space effort can also suppress a significant number of research opportunities. Whenever NASA or DOD enters a new field, it no longer remains profitable for private R&D to stay around. The inability of entrepreneurs to compete with public R&D planning has probably squandered many valuable opportunities. Moreover, when public plans are later aborted, it is too difficult for private firms to move back into what might have been a promising field of endeavor. The need for caution in planning R&D priorities and programs remains imperative.

THE INEVITABILITY
OF PLANNING

ROBERT LEKACHMAN

LATER IN THIS ESSAY, I shall describe the definition of planning implicit in the Humphrey–Hawkins full employment bill and the Humphrey–Javits national economic planning bills. These measures were halted in 1977 but they are certain to reappear in some new form in the next few years.

At the outset it is sufficient to borrow Leonard Silk's ecumenical formulation of the many meanings attached to the concept. In his words, "The term 'national planning' has a wide variety of meanings, ranging from the provision of more information and long-range forecasts by government to programs involving detailed allocation of resources and investment under government guidance and control."[1] Silk observes that "virtually all businessmen sympathetic to the planning idea are found at the mild and noninterventionist end of the spectrum." If such distinguished business leaders as Henry Ford II, J. Irwin Miller, W. Michael Blumenthal, Robert Roosa, and Felix Rohatyn have uttered words of interest or praise for planning, it clearly has been because they contemplate, still following Silk, a "system that would preserve capitalism,

Robert Lekachman is Distinguished Professor of Economics at Lehman College of the City University of New York.

[1] See his recently published *Ethics and Profits* (New York: Simon & Schuster, 1976), p. 49.

leave the control of the means of production largely in private hands, and keep capital accumulation and investment by corporations as the driving force of the economy—but with better coordination and long-range direction to meet national goals."

It is fair to draw a parallel between current support of planning by a minority of important business leaders and somewhat similar reactions of their predecessors of the 1930s to the New Deal. Although business opposition to Franklin Roosevelt (particularly after 1936) was very strong, such industrialists as Averell Harriman glimpsed in Social Security, farm supports, even the ill-conceived National Industrial Recovery Act, a potential reinforcement of the American version of market capitalism. One might even term this the natural Tory response to the inadequacies of given institutions—prudent reform to prevent violent change.

The crisis of the 1930s centered on mass unemployment in the Western European countries and the United States and the inadequacy of conventional economic responses. In Britain, a socialist Chancellor of the Exchequer, Philip Snowden, lamented in his memoirs that none of his economic advisers at the Treasury had told him that he could go off the gold standard and devalue the pound as an alternative to sharp budget cuts and counterproductive attempts to balance the budget. In 1930 and 1931, John Maynard Keynes, not yet the author of *The General Theory of Employment, Interest and Money,* was simply an unsound fellow who advocated dangerous deficit spending on public works.

In due course, Keynesian emphasis upon aggregate demand and Keynesian prescriptions for its stimulation during recession became the conventional wisdom of the younger and more alert members of the Roosevelt administration, such as Lauchlin Currie and Walter Salant.[2] But by 1964 so respectable a business organ as *Business Week* was hailing the Kennedy–Johnson $10 billion tax cut, at a time of mild recovery *and* existing deficit, as the triumph of an idea and the culmination of a successful experiment in economic management. In death if not in life, Keynes had been co-opted as a respectable agent of economic stability and business prosperity.

In the 1970s the economic crisis is much less calamitous in its human effects than its predecessor, in good part because of the protections built

---

[2] I tell this story briefly in *The Age of Keynes* (New York: McGraw-Hill, 1966), ch. 5.

into the American and other economies by the New Deal and its Western European analogues, among them unemployment compensation, food stamps, Medicare and Medicaid, and so on. In the United States the continuation of the New Deal by the Great Society supplemented Social Security not alone by food stamps and medical assistance but by a variety of housing and manpower programs.[3] Moreover, all governments react sooner and more vigorously to recession and unemployment than they did in the 1930s, because after Keynes no unresponsive government is likely to stay in office during a spell of stormy economic weather.

The very social programs and Keynesian techniques of economic manipulation which so many businessmen formerly opposed with great sincerity and vehemence have softened class conflict and promoted social harmony. It does not, I think, overstate Keynes's significance to conclude that Western Europe, Japan, Canada, Australia, New Zealand, and the United States enjoyed a generation of rising living standards after World War II because Keynesian economic policy in all those countries (whether avowed or not) kept recessions short and shallow and averted another Great Depression. The major exception to this generalization, Great Britain, was a society which for a variety of historical circumstances—a flagging of managerial initiative, a failure to adjust educational policy to the requirements of a technological society, and a persistence of class hostility, among others—failed to combine high rates of employment with reasonable rates of growth. In the United States the growth dividend each year was distributed widely enough among the general population to create the pleasant expectation that the ordinary person could in his own lifetime anticipate higher and higher real income. In England, where this growth dividend was small, zero, or at times negative, the struggle for increased income took on the desperation of a zero-sum game in which worker gains could be achieved only at the expense of capitalist losses.

To many observers, myself among them, the crisis of the 1970s and the accompanying failure of Keynesian solutions are linked to a series of changes that put in serious question the continuation of the combination

[3] An excellent appraisal of the successes and failures of these initiatives is supplied by Sar Levitan and Robert Taggart, *The Promise of Greatness* (Cambridge: Harvard Univ. Press, 1972).

of steady growth and improving living standards which has until recently made life in capitalist societies tolerable at least and highly satisfactory at best. The symbol of these adverse developments has been Paul Samuelson's rather ugly coinage, stagflation—the persistence for several years in this country and elsewhere of high rates of unemployment and inflation as though in flat defiance of Phillips curve trade-offs between the two. In the United States, living standards have slightly declined for average factory and office workers since 1973.

This decline in turn has dampened consumer spending, has reduced incentives for capital investment (well into the second year of recovery from the 1974–1975 mini-depression, American manufacturers were operating their factories at well below 80 percent of their capacity), and has pushed an increasing percentage of women into the labor force. It is one thing for a married woman to seek the satisfactions and status of professional success. It is quite another to seek any available job as necessary supplement to the declining real wages of one's husband. The otherwise puzzling increase in female labor-force participation in 1976 is, translated into these terms, quite easy to understand. Not women's lib but the exigency of tight family budgets was the responsible agent.

For several strong reasons I believe that the problems of this decade provide more than a passing difficulty. The manifest failure of conventional techniques of monetary and fiscal management relate, to begin with, to adverse turns in the market for energy and food. It is well to be clear about the role of OPEC. Cartels, according to conventional economic wisdom, are supposed to collapse within relatively brief periods because of increasing stress and incompatibility of purpose among the members of the cartel. Of this comforting hypothesis, it need only be said that OPEC shows no signs of disintegration and every mark of determination to continue its profitable supervision of the market for petroleum. The $30–35 billion which OPEC oil now costs Americans in excess of the 1973 price level represents a transfer of resources from Americans to foreigners, a subtraction from the fruits of economic growth, and a commensurate reduction of potential improvements in standards of life.

Energy is not likely to become cheaper in the future or, to put the matter somewhat differently, it will be necessary to devote more resources in future years to energy production than in past years. North

Sea and North Slope oil are expensive oil. Quite apart from its hazards to health and environment, nuclear energy has not fulfilled its early promise of low cost. Fusion, thirty or forty years in the future, may be the answer. It is a long time for most men and women now alive to wait. Most scientists discount solar energy and other still more exotic substitutes for fossil and nuclear sources.

On the face of it, one might think that the sharp and probably continuing increase in the world demand for food, stemming from demography as well as Russian efforts to improve diet, represented for Americans a balance-of-payments answer to adverse changes in energy. American agriculture, the marvel of the world, is quite probably the most efficient sector of the American economy. As the world's leading grain and soybean exporter, the United States has become the residual grocer of the globe. For the average American, however, the increasing importance of world markets to American farmers is scarcely an unmixed blessing. When the family supermarket bill rises with world demand, the vast urban majority of Americans face declining real earnings. The beneficiaries are a minority—farmers and food processors. At the same time that American food exports ameliorate imbalances in our international accounts, they also generate internal income transfers that threaten the prosperity of most Americans and the stability of the domestic economy.

Nor is this by any means the end of the sad tale of current difficulty. We perforce live at a time when older and simpler economic objectives come into increasing conflict with new values. A generation ago, perhaps even as recently as a decade ago, economists and laymen alike were content to take the growth of the Gross National Product as a reflection of improvement in economic welfare. Life for all of us, the business community notably included, has become far more complicated and even ambiguous. A spate of legislation and court interpretation has in a ten-year span imposed upon businessmen the responsibility to deal justly with women and minorities in their hiring and promotion practices. Affirmative action programs add to the expenses of personnel administration. Failure to abide by such programs leads to financial penalties of growing severity.

The new Occupational Safety and Health Act, which has gotten off to a stumbling administrative start, codifies a great many practices that responsible employers have long followed, but it also imposes in many cases costly capital expenditures and expensive record keeping. Environmental legislation imposes new responsibilities upon the operators of old plants and places substantial barriers in the path of utilities and energy corporations which seek to undertake new ventures. The consumer movement has generated a spate of laws applying in particular to automobiles, foods, and drugs, some of which retard the pace of innovation and all of which add measurably to costs.

Let it be plain that my own sympathies are in general with the partisans of civil rights, sexual and racial equality, product reliability, occupational health and safety, and environmental protection. When a major corporation can be found guilty of dumping kepone into a river and damaging the health of workmen in a closely affiliated company, an airline can ignore warnings about the reliability of a freight hatch door, and a pharmaceutical supplier can market, after inadequate testing, a drug whose use leads to the birth of sadly deformed infants, the case for more effective government supervision is difficult to rebut. However conscientious the management of a company, the dictates of profit are a standing temptation to cut corners on safety precautions, testing, and other expensive and time-consuming activities.

There can be no doubt, however, that these new and appropriate social responsibilities of business retard the growth of the Gross National Product, at least by conventional measures. It is a defect of national income accounting that its categories do not record as enhanced value the improved resistance to serious accident of new autos, the superior quality of air and water after antipollution measures have been taken, and like benefits from the new wave of consumer protections. The defect is more than the economists' and statisticians' alone. Few sellers advertise the benefits of the products marketed in compliance with new health and environmental regulations. Few consumers, accordingly, have fully appreciated the benefits as well as the costs of product reform.

Probably the least measurable of the international forces impinging on growth prospects in the industrialized West and Japan is the rising clamor by Third World nations for global redistribution. Very fortunate Third World countries that are rich in oil, and slightly less lucky nations with bauxite, tin, copper, chrome, or other useful materials, have taken redistribution into their own hands. Nations unendowed by Allah or other deities with strategic materials are clamoring for commodity agreements, grants or loans on concessionary terms, larger tax payments from multinational corporations, and other transfers from the rich to the poor. The terms of global competition between ourselves and the Russians and, to some extent, the Chinese make it highly likely that some portion of the banquet sought by the developing countries will be served to them, again at the price of some increment to possible growth in the United States and countries in a similar position.

This rapid tour of the horizon terminates in a single point. Contemporary economics works well or at least has worked well when growth is rapid enough to improve living standards and relax social and class tensions. It is manifestly helpless in a time of (probable) slow growth. It is a misfortune that, to borrow Thomas Kuhn's useful metaphor, there is no handy intellectual paradigm to guide us onto a stormy sea, much as the Keynesian paradigm came to the rescue of economists and politicians four decades ago. As a mild optimist, I hope that a powerful new intellectual construction will soon be advanced by the sort of original mind needed to make sense out of present confusion.

Since in the meantime life and politics go on, the best that can be done is to bring to bear the social intelligence, the organized rationality, and the conscious guidance of events which are implicit in serious attempts at even mildly interventionist planning, some of which (without saying so) this country has already experienced, and many of which surely lie in the future.

The American Planning Experience

Otis Graham at Stanford has traced the history of American planning back to Bernard Baruch's World War I War Industries Board.[4] Others of Graham's milestones include the New Deal National Resources Planning Board, Roosevelt initiatives in regional planning (the Tennessee Valley Authority) and sectoral planning (the two Agricultural Adjustment Acts, federal housing legislation, and the National Recovery Administration), the War Production Board and allied agencies during World War II, and the enactment in 1946 of the Employment Act.[5] Price and wage controls

[4] See Graham's *Toward a Planned Society* (New York: Oxford Univ. Press, 1976).

[5] Considerably exaggerating the significance of the Employment Act (which did no more than state the importance of "maximum" employment and establish in the Council of Eco-

reappeared during the Korean War and, rather startlingly, during the Nixon years.[6] It is worth recalling that when in August 1971 President Nixon suddenly froze wages and prices and later moved to Phase II or regulated changes, much of the business community was clamoring loudly for just such action. In the initial phase at least, the Nixon control program was highly popular.

Thus American experiments with planning have been discontinuous responses (with the partial exception of the Nixon program) to emergencies. The sort of planning which shapes actual producing, investing, consuming, and employment decisions—candidly interventionist national action—has been associated either with a major war or a deep depression. Military emergencies evoke, as their clear and focused objective, victory over the enemy. Detailed meddling by the bureaucrats has generally been publicly accepted as the necessary prerequisite of early triumph and, in any case, a smaller sacrifice than that borne by members of the armed services. Military emergencies are fortunately temporary. Thus at the conclusion of each war in this century the control apparatus has been summarily dismantled, usually to the accompaniment of considerable economic and political disarray. By January 1, 1919 the War Industries Board was out of business. As Graham tells the story, Bernard Baruch himself led the drive for early termination of his agency. A canny politician, he was too proud of the War Industry Board's reputation to risk damaging it after the armistice had been signed. In 1946 Republican congressional victories signaled the demise of price, wage, and credit controls. From a planning standpoint, Vietnam was a war fought by stealth. Desperately seeking simultaneously to preserve cherished Great Society programs and to win the war in Southeast Asia, Lyndon Johnson never sought from Congress the control and tax legislation that were conventional in earlier conflicts.

Opponents of interventionist planning thus can make the plausible

nomic Advisers and the Joint Economic Committee of Congress two agencies shorn of operating and legislative authority), Arthur Miller in *The Modern Corporate State* (Westport, Conn.: Greenwood Press, 1976), asserts that "the positive state received its charter in 1946 when Congress enacted the Employment Act" (p. 92). By the positive state, Miller clearly means the planned state.

[6] Mr. Nixon's personal distaste for controls began with six unhappy months as a compliance attorney in 1942 with the Office of Price Administration.

case that such planning is alien to American custom and political practice save in situations of grave general danger, for the most part external. Indeed the New Deal may be used to strengthen rather than weaken this position, for its "planning" was more a matter of ad hoc improvisation than consistent design, and Congress grew so suspicious of the very word that by 1940 it had abolished the National Resources Planning Board.

Labels, however, tend to disguise reality. If one takes a closer look at the American past, it is plain that in its least threatening guise (data collection and forecasting) planning has steadily expanded in our lifetime in the administrations of Presidents of both parties.[7]

I quite deliberately perceive data collection as an act of planning because rarely, if ever, is the definition of the information sought, the population queried, and the uses made of new statistics, devoid of normative or political impact. Bureaucratic objectives, quite limited initially, are likely to be enlarged and transformed by the very information acquired. Quite possibly the federal response to the Arab oil embargo in 1973 and 1974 would have been greatly different if the Nixon administration had possessed accurate, independent data (beyond those provided by Exxon and other major energy producers) dealing with the size, distribution, and transportation of existing oil stocks. It is still more likely that the Russian grain robbery of summer 1972 would have been less successful if the Department of Agriculture had had timely, complete information on the trading activities of major grain dealers. With such information American farmers might have received a larger share and American grain traders a smaller share of the benefits from massive Soviet purchases.

Such venerable domestic economic indicators as the consumer price index and the rate of unemployment are anything but value-free. Include in the second measure discouraged workers and full-time equivalents for the partially employed, and unemployment rates would rise, according to AFL-CIO estimates, by 2 or 3 percent. Require sterner tests of actual job search, as labor-market specialists like Harvard's Martin Feldstein suggest, and unemployment rates will surely decline. The

[7] During the Nixon era, executive-branch reorganization greatly enlarged White House command of data from cabinet agencies and enhanced the capacity of the President to coordinate policy.

point is sufficiently important to justify two more illustrations. Federal Trade Commission attempts to compel large corporations to disclose profits by individual profit line will, if ultimately successful in the face of court challenge, unquestionably publicize some extremely high returns on a number of items and fan public criticism of "monopoly" and "extortion" of the public. Similar consequences might well flow from mandatory publication of compliance with Arab boycotts on the part of American banks and multinational corporations, something of an issue in the 1976 presidential campaign.

Congressional conservatives who have traditionally voted against larger appropriations for the Department of Commerce, the Bureau of the Census, and the Bureau of Labor Statistics, have behaved with considerable sophistication. New information is not frequently an inert mass. Someone tends to use it, and the conservative temper is inveterately suspicious of new activities. All the same, more data will be collected in the future than in 1976, although one may hope that redundancy and duplication will be reduced. The trend of the kinds of federal legislation and administrative regulation covering the topics earlier alluded to—everything from the environment to equal opportunity—is firmly in the direction of new mandatory revelation of commercial information, the very foundation of new statistical series and equally fresh opportunity for new regulatory intervention.

Federal capacity to contemplate and actually undertake the sort of interventionist planning that systematically influences prices, production patterns, and consumer spending, expands with the size and quality of the data base. It is no accident that Wassily Leontieff, the Nobel laureate economist who pioneered input/output analysis, is also cochairman of the Initiatives Committee for National Economic Planning; this private group of academics, union leaders, and businessmen engaged the support of Senators Humphrey and Javits for a planning measure which took shape in the 1975–1976 Congress as the Humphrey–Javits national economic planning bill (S. 380). Leontieff insistently emphasizes the necessity of gathering far more detailed data, industry by industry, as the essential prelude to discussion of national goals, guidance of the economy toward such goals, alteration of existing patterns of production, consumer expenditure, and distribution of income and wealth, selection of growth paths, and pursuit of other quantifiable goals.

More and better data have important consequences for the private planning which successful corporations routinely undertake. It is, or at least should be, self-evident that the larger the corporation, the more dependent for success it is upon accurate evaluation of national and international trends. Already publicly regulated, a utility like the operating companies of AT&T has little to lose and much to gain from diminished uncertainty about the shape of its market five or ten years hence. Successful business managers perforce plan for a mysterious future. Anything that diminishes the mystery ought, on grounds of self-interest, to be welcome. Nothing that has happened since 1936 diminishes the force of this classic Keynesian observation by a man who knew a great deal more about investment markets than most economists:

Our knowledge of the factors which will govern the yield of an investment some years hence is usually very slight and often negligible. If we speak frankly, we have to admit that our basis of knowledge for estimating the yield ten years hence of a railway, a copper mine, a textile factory, the good will of a patent medicine, an Atlantic liner, a building in the City of London amounts to little and sometimes to nothing. . . . Businessmen play a mixed game of skill and chance, the average results of which to the players are not known by those who take a hand.[8]

For this reason, among others, Keynes looked forward to what he called in a concluding chapter a "somewhat comprehensive socialisation of investment."

Forecasting

Data collection and data forecasting are very closely linked. Antiplanners are likely to judge forecasting as even more threatening than new statistics. More precisely, the antiplanners oppose extension of the very considerable quantity of public forecasting already routine in Washington. As best it can, the Treasury foretells tax collections and federal

[8] See John Maynard Keynes, *The General Theory of Employment, Interest and Money* (New York: Harcourt, 1936), pp. 149–50.

outlays eighteen months ahead. The Department of Agriculture issues
generally more accurate crop prophecies which enormously affect futures markets and food prices. Under a fresh congressional mandate, the
Council of Economic Advisers furnishes five-year perspectives on unemployment, GNP, productivity, and other interesting variables. The new
Congressional Budget Office uses much of its increasing staff to analyze
future revenues and outlays, as an alternative legislative Council of Economic Advisers or Department of the Treasury.

However honestly derived, a forecast of any significant economic
event or indicator is a tool of partisan politics. Consider for a moment
the Humphrey–Hawkins full employment bill, whose major elements
were explicitly and warmly endorsed by the 1976 Democratic platform
and more temperately by the Democratic candidate. The final version of
the bill in September 1976, just before congressional adjournment killed
it for that session, involved several planning elements. It required the
President to make a forecast each January of unemployment in the coming year on the basis of data collected in the executive branch. It contained two additional planning components which we shall briefly
discuss in the next two sections. First it enunciated a target or goal: the
bill required the President and Congress to attain within four years
3 percent adult unemployment or less. Adults were defined as men and
women twenty years of age or more. A goal of 3 percent adult unemployment implied a target of 4–4.5 percent general unemployment, for
unemployment among teenagers is notoriously high. The final planning
element, of course, was the mandate imposed jointly upon Congress and
the President to enact the spending and taxing measures required to
move the economy along its target path.

Very little imagination is required to identify the possibilities of partisan conflict. A Republican president confronted by a Democratic Congress, a familiar spectacle in the last generation, would be tempted to
offer Congress relatively cheerful forecasts of the coming year's economic performance and, therefore, little in the way of stimulus to activity. Argument would then focus on the accuracy of the forecast and the
adequacy of the program which the forecast legitimately generated.
Forecasts themselves are based on assumptions susceptible to challenge.
They are frequently offered as a range of values. It is the nature of politics and politicians to select single numbers at opposite ends of the range

and belabor one another with the number of their partisan preference. Planning, when it comes, will no doubt bear other names of sponsors than Humphrey, Javits, and Hawkins. The Carter administration, notably in its approach to energy, is clearly technocratic in its impulses.

National Goals

In the last generation several quite specific national goals were stated by Presidents and ratified by subsequent congressional action. One was President Eisenhower's interstate highway program, complete with trust fund and sequestered revenues from gasoline tax receipts. Another was John F. Kennedy's space program, which did indeed place a man on the moon within the decade he specified.

Americans are also familiar with much fuzzier and more general national goals—full employment, economic growth, revival of the cities, victory over cancer and strokes, increase in longevity, and so tiresomely on. By themselves, of course, national goals are no more than the sort of statement of warm aspiration that perennial Rockefeller commissions have published for a generation, usually in the context of suspicion that their sponsor was again running for president.

When goals are enunciated within the context of firm data and routine forecasting, they lack merely the pressure of political circumstance to facilitate much more active planning of an interventionist nature. It is worth emphasizing that the two planning measures which actually surfaced in Congress and public discussion took different attitudes toward goals. Humphrey–Hawkins flatly focused on full employment, harking back to the original full employment bill of 1945, which in drastically weakened form became the Employment Act of 1946. By contrast, Humphrey–Javits left the objectives of planning open to political argument, full employment amounting to only one of a cluster of possible objectives.

Interventionist Planning

As planning, American-style, is emerging into the daylight of respectable discussion among serious people, it seems to display four major characteristics. It is addressed above all to the formulation of consistent

goals. These goals, second, are decidedly not imposed from above as in
Soviet-style coercive planning. Soviet planning substitutes the preferences of the planners for those of the public. Western, democratic varie-
ties of planning in sharp contrast attempt to identify the preferences of
the public through the usual channels of public discussion, parliamen-
tary action, and group consultation. Again in contrast to coercive planning, a third characteristic of democratic planning is the nature of the
incentive system. Characteristically, Dutch, Swedish, and French
planners have jiggled tax, credit, contract, and trade structures with a
view to influencing the decisions of private businessmen in directions
consonant with the objectives of given plans. The rationality of profit
maximization is enlisted in the service of democratically approved goals.
And, finally, any planning effort which goes further than mere forecasting is likely to require, certainly in the United States, appropriate new
legislation, a new planning agency, and the revision and extension of existing data-collecting efforts.

The Humphrey–Javits national economic planning statute is politically
interesting because of its sponsorship by two mainstream liberals. Neither, in long and successful public careers, has ever strayed very far in
advance of his constituency. The measure itself, which perished with
congressional adjournment in early October 1976, embodies the mildest
possible version of interventionist planning. It mandates no planning
goals. Rather it requires the President to propose plans, Congress to
debate them and ultimately to enact in some version two- and six-year
plans for the economy, much like current arrangements according to
which Presidents propose federal budgets, Congresses alter them, and
ultimately a rough plan for the expenditure and financing of a quarter or
so of the GNP is made law.

Senate bill 380 did not prescribe any particular monetary or fiscal
strategy. Much less did it opt for incomes policy, credit allocation, and
other devices familiar not only to foreign planners but to Americans who
are old enough to recall World War II and subsequent events. Any, all,
or some of these and other devices might be recommended by a given
chief executive and accepted by his Congress; none is mandated. The
statutory language of S. 380 is sufficiently general and ambiguous that it
might almost be plausibly interpreted as only a short pace beyond the
coordinating activities of the existing Office of Management and Budget.

At most, S. 380 amounted to an invitation to a new set of political arguments and a legitimization of democratic planning as a future congressional option. A planning enthusiast might hope, but only hope, that passage of some revised version of S. 380 in the next Congress, in itself far from a certainty, might lead in the direction of policies already extensively experimented with, with varying degrees of success over varying periods of time, in Western Europe and Japan.

At the risk of redundancy, it is necessary to stress two points. Our European friends already deploy far more sophisticated trade, credit, manpower-training, land-use, and other policies than we currently employ. Yet, and this is the second point, none of these public interventions is unprecedented in American political and economic history. The novelty will be their role as part of a peacetime national economic plan. Thus critics and partisans of national economic planning are both correct when, disapprovingly or approvingly, they conclude that democratic planning in the United States will alter current relations between business and government and perceptibly modify traditional American preferences for solutions perceived as those of free markets to economic allocation.

One need scarcely note that planning contains no magic. Planning may accompany stagnation as in England. Equally it may be an ingredient of outstanding economic performance as in Sweden. It may work well at some times, as it once did in France. It may for complex reasons lose its credibility, as has apparently occurred in France during the last two or three years.

The Politics of Planning

I have already labeled S. 380 an invitation to political debate. Resolution of divergent views of appropriate goals, timetables, methods, and rewards and penalties will inevitably reflect existing distributions of power and influence among economic interest groups—farmers, large corporations, unions, small businessmen, and newer constituencies of minorities, environmentalists, and public-interest groups. We are all fortunate that the American political process is an unusually open clash of organized pressure groups. This said, I nevertheless translate my prediction that planning will reflect the distribution of power and influ-

ence into the judgment that when mildly interventionist planning comes
to the United States it will bear the clear fingerprints of our largest corporations and their allies in the legal and academic community. I would
judge that the corporate-legal-academic complex is the most potent of
interest groups in our conservative society.

Just because the United States lacks an organized Left of any consequence, alert business proponents of national economic planning are
fully justified in their tacit judgment that planning will protect corporate
prosperity and increase the stability of the mixed economy within which
corporations now operate.

No doubt democratic socialists and egalitarians like myself (an almost
invisible American political sect) would, given the chance, preside over
a planning process which drastically altered present allocations of income, wealth, and power. But I operate out of no delusion that Michael
Harrington, John Kenneth Galbraith, Robert Heilbroner, and myself
will shape the planning process.[9]

Yet is is dangerous to depend on catastrophe to serve one's own preferences and values. The Communists in the Weimar Republic who refused to join a common front against Hitler died in Hitler's
concentration camps. A radical in a conservative climate can never
forget that economic or political calamity is far more likely to serve the
purposes of the George Wallaces than of the Democratic Socialist
Organizing Committee. Hence there are at least three identifiable
merits for radicals in conservative, corporate-dominated planning. First,
even when intelligent conservatives dominate the political action, it is
better for average individuals and families that they govern rationally although the proceeds of rationality flow disproportionately to the rich and
the powerful. Intelligent conservatives are likely to recognize the neces-

---

[9] In Michael Harrington's most recent book, *The Twilight of Capitalism* (New York:
Simon & Schuster, 1974), he looks forward to a final crisis of capitalism followed by a version of democratic socialism which he somewhat cheerfully reads into the Marxist canon.

In *Economics and the Public Purpose* (Boston: Houghton, 1974), Galbraith describes
large corporations as prominent members of an already planned sector. He advocates a
mixture of nationalization and state intervention in the interests of redistribution that ap-
proximates, absent Harrington's final crisis, the same vision of pluralist planning.

Heilbroner's recent *Business Civilization in Decline* (New York: Simon & Schuster,
1976) interprets the likely shape of planning in the United States very much as I have
done. He too believes that planning will serve corporate interests and prolong the effective
career of capitalist institutions.

sity, in their own interest, of relatively high levels of employment and relatively decent programs of income maintenance and health care. Second, the sort of publicly open planning process with which our European friends have experimented since the end of World War II represents an opportunity for education and influence even on the part of relatively weak democratic socialists and left-wing liberals. Finally, an opening for progressive change does occur occasionally: Woodrow Wilson's New Freedom in 1913 and 1914, the first four years of Franklin Roosevelt's New Deal in the 1930s, and those *anni mirabili* of the Great Society, 1964–1966, before an unpopular war blighted the prospects of further progress at home. Progressive Presidents are aware that their opportunity to push through important legislation is historically short. Congress invariably reasserts itself. An ongoing planning capacity would improve the chance that future spells of political opportunity for the moderate Left will be used to maximum advantage. I must report, less as a reason than as an uneasy feeling, that the margins for national error are rapidly shrinking. As the prospects of quick growth diminish, recoveries are likely to be weaker and recessions deeper and more protracted, at least in the absence of better coordinated economic responses than we are presently equipped to make.

I am thus led back to the beginning of my argument. The world is an increasingly precarious speck in the universe. It is afflicted by resource shortages (natural or contrived), seemingly intractable population pressures, demands from the Third World for global redistributions of wealth, threats to the environment, background threats of nuclear incidents, and, of course, the persistent political competition of the Soviet Union. At home there are the nagging afflictions of unemployment, inflation, urban decay, maldistributed health care, inadequate housing, drug abuse, faltering education, and work dissatisfaction. It is increasingly apparent to political observers of many faiths that these and still other postindustrial dilemmas are interconnected. Solution of one may well aggravate others. The case for planning derives in the end from the need to coordinate plans for a wholesome environment *and* full employment, energy conservation *and* improving living standards, tax equity *and* adequate capital formation, and so on.

The case for planning does not demand that the planners be wiser or more altruistic than chairmen of the board. Nor will planning lead us

into some New Jerusalem on earth. No, planning is merely a better
response than uncoordinated, partly competitive markets to the problems of an ever more interdependent economy and ever more interdependent world.

I retain a modicum of faith in the strength and viability of American
democratic institutions, and in the residual good will that opposing
groups and interests bear toward one another. Although any observer of
the 1976 presidential contest might well be saddened by the failures of
the candidates to speak other than in the clichés of outmoded arguments, I hope and expect that in the next decade under administrations
of either party the American polity will grapple rationally with its neces-
sities. It is in that sense that I restate my belief that planning is inevitable.

A RESPONSE

Planning—Yes, But by Whom?

GORDON T. BOWDEN

ROBERT LEKACHMAN has presented an attractive argument for the inevitability of planning. He points out that support for planning, at least in a mild degree, exists among businessmen as well as among the academics and government staffers. He further points out that a trend toward planning has long historical roots in America, going back at least to World War I. He urges us to recognize the simple logic of this planning trend in an increasingly complex, developed society. He adds that the use of resources in a high-consumption society can lead to serious depletion or other misuse of natural resources without some centralized control.

Lekachman acknowledges that strong government intervention in economic life has occurred only in time of war or other national crisis. Nevertheless, in peaceful periods we have been moving steadily toward more and more government intervention in economic activity. The momentum given to planning by President Roosevelt and the Democratic party has continued to the present. This movement shows itself in the growing academic and bureaucratic appetite for the collection of data by government agencies and the growing development of forecasting techniques, not to mention the growing disposition to impose regulation in more areas of everyday life.

Gordon T. Bowden is Director of Educational Relations in the Public Relations and Employee Information Department at American Telephone and Telegraph.

The need for centralized planning is typically presented by its advocates with the beguiling argument that technological innovations have made our lives so complex and the economy so large that it cannot, without regulation, serve the needs of all the people (to twist a popular cliché) "with equality and justice for all." As the argument goes, the uncoordinated activities of millions of individuals and organizations in such a large, rapidly changing economy, create unemployment and dislocation problems that unfairly impose themselves more on some groups than on others. The punch line is that the activities of all these self-seeking individuals and groups need a referee, and that that referee must be the government.

A variation of this argument from the more idealistic planners is that, given the quality of human nature, if people are left to themselves they will not do the things that should be done for all people in a society. The government must therefore take the initiative to do these socially desirable things for all the people.

These pressures of growth and these socioeconomic aspirations have made it seem more and more that some kinds of government planning are inevitable. In addition to the minimal planning for national defense, foreign relations, the currency, immigration, courts and law enforcement, we have come to accept an extension of this idea into the areas of health, education, and welfare, and labor relations. We have accepted the need for some government planning in the protection of our industries from the economic effects of foreign products and foreign labor entering our markets. No one can seriously argue that we have not raised the standard of living or the quality of life as the role of government has become more prominent. But we can question how much of it is the result of governmental or centralized planning.

Two points which have already received some discussion need to be emphasized. First, it is easy to agree that some kinds of planning are desirable, maybe inevitable in everyday life, but a critical question is, Planning by whom? Planning by the federal government on a national scale has certain consequences; planning by private businesses and individuals has quite different results. This is a key issue of great concern to us and should be to those who work in the academic world.

It is of concern to us because we see that present government efforts to plan how communications shall be provided in this country have interfered with the planning and performance efforts of communications companies. It should be of concern to academic people because growing federal aid to education can destroy local control of education in the public as well as the private sector.

I am not going to recite here the reasons why we believe a new determination of communications policy is needed. Obviously, in supporting the Consumer Communications Reform Act, we believe that regulation of network common carriers for communications services is in the public interest. Other kinds of regulation may or may not be in the public interest in many other industries. But regulation and planning are not and need not be the same.

And this is my second point. *Regulations* should be no more than guidelines and requirements to assure that the public interest is protected in the normal conduct of everyday affairs. As such, regulations should not dictate how any industry shall develop except in the broadest terms, and only in areas not covered by laws already on the books. The directions of technological innovation, the costs of products and services in relation to rate of return, the rate of growth, the opportunity to succeed or fail in pricing optional services, are all aspects of economic activity that, as far as possible, should be left to the interactions and exchange transactions of the market. Standards of service, quality of products, safety of products and services should be monitored not by inexperienced, cause-minded staff people but rather through guidelines worked out and accepted as reasonable by the industry.

Planning, on the other hand, is an activity important to every individual and organization with a contribution to make to the life of society. The magnitude and variety of these activities is so tremendous that no central authority could acquire or manage the information needed to plan them in the public interest. Technology can be planned on a very large scale, but human beings are not robots and their behavior resists the technical rigidities of system and bureaucratic process that are essential to planning. Lekachman says that "planning does not demand that the planners be wiser or more altruistic than chairmen of the board." I think that national planning does require more wisdom—altruism may be irrelevant. Planning wisdom at the corporate level has been hard enough to find without seeking sufficient wisdom to engage in national planning. Even the most ardent advocates of this kind of plan-

ning—the Russians—have had to back away from playing God in recent
years.

Planners often ask: But how can the public interest be served without
government planning when very large corporations dominate large areas
of economic activity? AT&T is often cited as a prime example. It is assumed by some planners that in the communications business there is
no way for the consumer to exert any influence on the supplier. In reality, through regulatory commissions, the telephone consumer can exert
more influence than a consumer in many nonregulated businesses. The
telephone consumer has access to state commissions and the FCC by
registering a complaint which the commission is obliged to investigate.
Thus his complaint gets more attention than does the complaint of the
buyer of an automobile, a refrigerator, or a dishwasher. The skeptics are
usually not satisfied with this. They further argue that the utility commissions, through insufficient knowledge, cannot make comprehensive
appraisals of the communication technology and economics and therefore cannot control for the public interest. This is an argument that
makes sense only if we expect the commissions to judge aspects of management that should be left to management.

From a business point of view the prospects of government agencies
trying to develop enough information about economic activity to make
federal planning possible is as alarming as the prospect of federal planning itself. The cost of such a data-collection program, to say nothing of
the misuses to which it might be put, make the Humphrey–Javits and
Humphrey–Hawkins bills sound like nightmares we should vigorously
oppose.

The bare-bones functions of government in protecting us from ene-
mies, "foreign and domestic," already require knowledge that we cannot
yet acquire in sufficient amounts to handle them effectively. How much
more difficult it would be to obtain the tremendously greater knowledge
to fully regulate the economy. The Federal Reserve and the Treasury,
along with the large spending agencies of HEW and Labor, have shown
us how difficult governmental intervention is in their limited spheres,
and their track record in their respective areas should give the most en-
thusiastic national planners substantial pause.

There are some who are not deterred by these prospects. They like to argue that these large special-interest groups cannot be depended on to act in the public interest unless coerced by some central authority to do so. The only solution, they argue, is to force these special interests to make the necessary concessions and to collaborate. In the absence of a threat of war or collapse in the economy, it is difficult to see how such a collaboration could be forced. Moreover, even if possible, how valuable would such a forced collaboration be? Its cost in policing activity would be astronomical. The costs of regulation are already very large. Such an approach would further weaken the accommodation that now tends to exist below the national level among the multitude of interest groups, arrived at through open exchanges of information and free determination of goals. This may be the only viable way to carry on everyday economic, political, and social life in a dynamic, democratic society.

With the coercion that is unavoidable in a planned society, and the elaborate processes required for data collection and control regulations, the economic consequences of planning tend to be hidden or disguised for idealistic reasons. When their cumulative effects appear, it is difficult to cope with them without more planning and coercion. In a complex society, timely economic feedback at all levels is crucial. National planning interferes with this because of its bureaucratic strictures.

A common response of planners to this kind of analysis is to abandon logic and appeal to romantic emotions by saying the private sector view of planning is cold and lacking in humane consideration for the poor, the little guy, and the otherwise disadvantaged people. The history of national planning, when it has been attempted on that level, shows that it hurts these groups more than it helps them in the long run. Even drastic income redistribution cannot help all groups equally over a given period of time. Inevitably the equalizing actions are destroyed by the necessary economic trade-offs between people, and immediately some will have more than others. The works of Eli Ginzberg, Edward Banfield, Daniel Patrick Moynihan, Christoper Jencks, and Irving Kristol all attest to the futility of overplanning at the federal level.

In sum, the interest in equality of opportunity which is a key feature in the planner's outlook is an Achilles heel that evolves too easily into an obsession with equality of results. The scale of personal manipulation and coercion called for to achieve equality of results is beyond imagination, and the attempt to achieve it in economic or social conditions leads to repressive measures that have no end—often with the intellectuals becoming one of the first groups to suffer.

So I appeal to those from the academic community as well as those in business to support the distinction between national planning, with its unwieldy rigidities, and private sector planning where timely feedback of consequences can provide a steadying power impossible at the governmental level. This distinction should be coupled with the idea of minimal regulation and minimal government intervention in economic activity. In those situations where broad exceptions should be made for the protection of the public interest, legislative determinations are better than agency regulations. Although we accept both legislative and agency regulation for communications services, a case could be made for legislative policy and court rulings without agency intervention. But the public may not be ready for that. In our claim that competition is not in the public interest for the national communications network, we do not presume that there are no other similar business situations, simply that the nature of the service should determine public action.

Discussion

Planning as Ideology and Strategy

ELI GINZBERG. I want to find a middle ground between the opposing positions that have been presented. Thirty-five years of exposure to the federal government persuades me that political movement in Washington is neither as rational nor as harmful as ideological advocates argue. On one side it is evident that powerful planning instruments are already in place and that their use by government can be enormous. But it must also be recognized that the linkages and mechanisms of power are so complex that no one knows how to control the machinery adeptly; nor does anyone know what consequences will flow from its use. I hope that the studies of the Congressional Budget Office will help us at last to sort out the strategic choices, the opportunity costs, and the policy outcomes that result from government planning. But I would not hold out too high a hope.

In the field that I know best, manpower legislation, the Congress has repeatedly called for action from HEW, the Department of Labor and OMB. But to call comes easily, to implement action does not. The overlapping jurisdiction of federal and state agencies confuses rational planning; so, too, do the conflicting constituencies of each agency. Moreover, the flow of information on which the Congress must rely is so limited that it cannot be bold in policy innovation. With the best will in the world, its injunctions must be cautious so long as the machinery for policy planning remains faulty and cumbersome.

Nor can the second-order problems of economic planning be ignored. Even if we knew more about the fine-tuning of the system of government planning, we still do not know whether movements in the whole economic system can be accurately gauged. For example, will a manpower outlay of $10 billion generate serious inflationary conse-

quences, will it delay investment expansion by corporate industry, or
will it genuinely improve the income earned by the work force? There is
a margin for error in these estimates that no planner can ignore.

The functional linkage between government information systems and
policy planning has long been appreciated. Unfortunately, the scarcity of
good information deflects the ambitions of even the toughest of leaders.
When Kennedy first entered the White House he asked Cabinet
members to submit reports to him twice a week. When they complied,
his administration almost ground to a halt. Department heads spent half
of their week in formulating exhaustive reports while the President had
to fight his way through the piles of memos accumulating on his desk.
He eventually realized that it was better to leave the machinery of government to grind forward, however badly, than to design a new system
of information gathering and policy planning. His preference for small-
step action over grandiose strategy reflected a realistic conclusion: that
planning energies and ambitions have to be conserved if government is
ever to be creative and vigorous.

FRANKLIN LONG. An element of ideological confusion lingers in most
discussions about planning. Management in the private sector rejects
the appeal for central planning even though corporate staffs practice it
assiduously. On the other hand, public officials are called upon by
Congress to defend their judgment in long-range plans or program design; yet they relegate planning functions to relatively junior staff levels
in the table of bureaucratic organization. Even academic theorists who
poke fun at fears of Big Brother in the front office are reluctant to concede a role for management planning in the administration of their university. Practical experience, it seems, does not diminish theoretical
commitments.

The confusion in ideology is matched by the disorder in planning
data. For example, the decision to create a federal Council for Science
and Technology was based on the assumption that shared interests
would link the Department of Defense, the National Science Foundation, and the Atomic Energy Commission. It was never known whether
there were good reasons to share and coordinate the research interests
of these agencies; or if there were wastages in their use of resources that
could be eliminated. The new council was supposed to define program

goals and budget priorities, but it lacked the political clout to translate scientific priorities into authoritative, manageable options. For its part, private industry claims to follow a discipline dictated by profit-and-loss calculations; but this is not a good substitute for strategic planning. Short-run market research can not replace the programmatic and rationalizing impulses in the public sector for which Robert Lekachman has called in his enthusiasm for central planning.

RICHARD WILSON. Rationalizing impulses are obviously of public concern, but they must be distinguished from normative or reformist impulses. The problem of distinguishing between them is critically important. Private sector industry has to manage its own internal planning, but it also has to follow the reformist ambitions and the fluctuating constraints imposed by a succession of political leaders. The result is often disastrous. The parameters of competition are usually known with some accuracy within each industrial sector, but the exercise of government regulations remains uncertain and can be illogical. Clearly, there can be no rationalizing thrust when one sector operates under the restraints of a market system while the other remains politically unpredictable.

The private sector today is obliged to meet the expectations that are set for it by a competitive, mass market. But it must also support the tax burdens and the regulatory codes that are devised by bureaucratic zealots, inexperienced legislators, and well-meaning outsiders. Industry finds no difficulty in working with such clear-cut and reasonable measures as Social Security or workmen's compensation. It discovers that public planning is an excessive burden only when government intervenes clumsily or inequitably to impede the efficient working of the market mechanism. In short, if we believe in the autonomy of a competitive market, it is logical that industry should be free to reach for an optimum level of efficiency. In this manner, industry can fulfill its own missions as well as those of the society it serves.

CARL HORN. A further word must be added regarding the planning impulses that are supposed to distinguish the public from the private economy. So long as we hope to maintain a democratic or open society, we must preserve the difference between macroeconomic and microeconomic controls. At the macro level we usually agree about the value of controlling inflation, maintaining full employment and a fair distribution of income. But it is in the realm of microeconomics that care must be taken to respect the operating needs of each industry or individual firm. If they are all lumped together into great planning categories or regulatory codes, they will never achieve the effective performance that the public sector anticipates. Public agencies cannot possibly replace the wealth-generating efficiency of the market. The best thing they can do is to leave it to operate as freely as it can.

Planning: Setting Goals and Priorities

DAVID APTER. Rationality has been invoked as a characteristic mode of the planning process. Desirable as this expectation might be, it must be supplemented with a high degree of political intelligence if planning is to materialize as a pragmatic rather than an ideological exercise. Poor planning or no planning can only generate chaos in a society as intricate as our own. Alternatively, partial or limited attempts at planning tend to enhance the power of limited or specialized interests. In short, bureaucratic half-measures are more likely to benefit the users or the producers of power than to protect the general welfare. The flow of political intelligence must therefore be seen as a major determinant of the responsiveness of government, of the responsibility of power groups, and of the welfare benefits that are distributed in our society.

The concept of "rationality" implies that political mechanisms will correct abuses of intelligence in predicting social change and regulating economic growth. Political parties are expected to help define the priorities of government or to realign policy programs with contemporary economic needs. Their failure to do so can be measured by the information feedback that they ought to provide but rarely succeed in doing. At election time, party leaders distort intelligence for ideological purposes, and they give inadequate concern to the correction of abuses or institutional errors. The rationality of the political system is diminished to the extent that party leaders resort to demagoguery rather than to the rational formulation of policy goals or alternative, programmatic choices.

Unfortunately, our electoral and legislative cycles are fundamentally out of phase with the planning cycles of economic or social change. There is a hit-or-miss quality in the phasing of planning initiatives. As Eli Ginzberg noted, Keynesian measures to expand employment too often conflict with inflationary spirals in the economy or with destabiliz-

ing trends in the balance of payments. Countries as diverse as Britain
and Italy, one enjoying a stable mode of government and the other not,
have tried to plan public policy on a counter-cyclical basis. Due to faulty
political intelligence, and to defects in the bureaucratic mechanism,
they generated stop–go "stagflation" rather than balanced economic
growth.

Socialist leaders recognize the difficulties in predicting and controlling
the rate of change in a capitalist economy. In many countries they have
utilized political intelligence to articulate accurate and perceptive criti-
cisms of the capitalist economy. But in all too few countries have they
succeeded in correcting the defects of the market or creating new social
programs. Arguably, central planning has not worked well in either
Western or Eastern Europe in recent years. It has failed to implement
the "reformist impulses" of socialist movements or to match the increase
in productivity scored by capitalist regimes. Although socialist parties
have helped secure a redistribution of income and transfer payments,
they have achieved few successes in planning for social or economic
growth.

MURRAY WEIDENBAUM. The discussion of the virtues and alleged neces-
sities of planning in American society must focus on two critical issues:
What are the system consequences and who gains (or who loses) in the
planning process?

The poor record of central planning mechanisms has already been
noted. One point deserves to be stressed. The emphasis of Mr. Carter
on alleviating unemployment is deeply suffused with wishful thinking. It
ignores, as did the Humphrey–Hawkins bill, the inflationary consequences of deficit spending at a point when the federal deficit is already at an all-time high. This intellectual omission is more serious than
the limitations of data or the cumbersome bureaucracy with which government must work. If planners ignore long-term outcomes in order to
secure short-term political gains, the costs of bad planning will be
greater than those of not planning.

Second, we cannot ignore the roles of big business, big labor, and big
government in determining policy programs or economic priorities. It is
the individual worker or consumer who suffers when powerful organizations gain. In the most controlled of industries, such as defense procurement, small and medium firms find it too expensive to do business with

government. Procurement officials are readily seduced by working in-
timately with big companies; they expect that considerable time and
overhead expense will be wasted in the process of bidding on large contracts. Avoiding the excessive time and cost commitments entailed in
defense business has not been permitted; small and medium firms have
therefore removed themselves from competitive bidding. This has hurt
both the efficiency of the defense industries and the employment opportunities that smaller companies could offer.

ROBERT GILPIN. We appear to be using three different interpretations
of a key word. "Planning" is first used to refer to the *tools* available to
government in extending traditional contols over fiscal or industrial policy, both at the macro- and micro-levels. Second, we talk about planning
in the newly found *coordination* within government or between the
public and the private sectors. Third, there is a normative connotation;
this stresses the *desirability,* if not the feasibility, of instituting an incomes policy or of redistributing social payments and consumer powers.

The last interpretation is the most controversial of the three categories. We have come to view planning in the first or instrumental
sense, or even in the second (as a coordination of public and private policy) as if it were politically neutral in meaning. Neither use of the term
is supposed to provoke institutional or class conflicts; both suggest a
promise to expand the total pie that is to be divided within American society. I find the asumption of neutrality to be unacceptable.

In an era of falling growth rates and increasing economic austerity, we
have begun to look at the third category in a more controversial or politically divisive interpretation. Egalitarian or reformist impulses, merely
by redistributing social payments or consumer power, reduce other
groups' privileges. As a result, the debate over central planning has
become more intensely politicized than at any time (at least for the
United States) since the New Deal. We now argue more heatedly over
this third interpretation when we talk about a future for New York and
the decaying cities of the Northeast. Our political divisions are beginning to focus more anxiously upon "dividing the spoils," with something
of the rancor of the electoral disputes seen in Western Europe.

WILLIAM BETTERIDGE. In this context the distinction must be made between planning as a tool of management and as a vehicle of public con-

trol. Industry knows how to manage its own organizational affairs, but there are no comparable techniques for the public control of social resources. Instead of agreeing upon social objectives and instrumental costs, we tend to plan simply by bargaining short-term trade-offs among competing groups. The result is not a plan but a patchwork of deals between the strong and the weak, or between managers in the public and private sectors. So long as the American economy remains rich and dynamic, the planning process will maintain an open-ended and democratic pluralism. But in terms of systematic resource management, it will also maintain an incoherent game plan.

RICHARD WILSON. Unfortunately, there is a price to pay for this planless incoherence. It is paid in a regressive redistribution of cost burdens by the lower-income consumer. This has been the worst outcome as far as the Bell System is concerned. The Communications Act of 1934 set out the operating rules that AT&T had to follow in allocating the costs necessary to provide a universal network of services. Now that we have to face competition in the connection of equipment and in intercity services, we might have to reduce the subsidy built into mass, low-cost, residential telephone rates. This outcome was neither anticipated by the government nor widely welcomed.

If AT&T is to create the technologically complex system that society will require over the next twenty years, it must plan today how best to raise billions of dollars in new capital. It cannot resign itself to a paternalist intervention of government. But neither can it meet an increase in intercity competition and at the same time fulfill the capital- and the technical-expansion programs, for which expensive funding is required, without price restructuring. It may be unable to avoid raising residential rates, regressively, to fulfill these conflicting obligations to society. As a nationwide utility, AT&T might find that it has no choice but to pass through to millions of customers the cost burdens added by government policy. That does not appear to be a rational outcome for the planning process.

The Politics of Planning

ANDREW HACKER. In my opening paper I suggested that our national character is the product of our unique national history. I return to this

theme in closing in order to stress the element of anarchy that is evident
in the American character. It has resisted direction and planning just as
it has resisted would-be dictators and theoretical ideologies.

Murray Weidenbaum has recounted the multitude of errors committed
by government in its efforts at regulation and control. But he failed to
recognize that government in this country was supposed to be awful! It
was built on the premise that government institutions should be inept,
toothless, inefficient, and filled with second-rate people.

Nor can I agree with David Apter's notion that planning arrangements
in our society require an organized rationality. The New Rationality, as I
put it in my paper, rejects such subtle theoretical constructs. (Moreover, by capitalizing the phrase, I meant to cast doubt on the ear-
nestness of its intention.) It is based on the ability to muddle through
new challenges and to adapt to new life styles without benefit of predic-
tive formulae. I am confident that we will adjust to the dire scarcities
and the economic hardships that have been foreseen in future years. We
will of course talk about social idealism, the redistribution of income,
and the ending of poverty. But if we should actually take action, we will
be sure to leave the structure of American capitalism intact. Indeed,
though political criticism might become as irritating as mosquito biting,
I still see a glorious future for AT&T and its corporate colleagues. As a
long-term investment it can only prosper.

Admittedly, protest and dissatisfaction will increase as our economic
promise begins to pall; we will probably see a rising tide of complaints,
impatience, and demoralization. There is nothing in the laws of God, nature, or history that dictates the survival of America's preeminence.
Other nations have successfully survived the course of economic decline, and I am confident that we can endure the experience, too. We
will struggle to protect our particular interests and to conserve our considerable wealth. But I doubt that we will resort to comprehensive planning to reverse the historical decline toward which we are now
speeding.

DAVID APTER. I cannot accept your complacent vision of decline. It may
be true that there are admirable traits in our national character, but I
am not sure that Americans will be able to adjust as stolidly to the
course of austerity as you suggest. In fact, I find your theory of political
survival to be remarkably uncompelling.

You foresee that millions of people now living in poverty, and possibly additional millions who are yet to join them, will resign themselves to permanent deprivation without resorting to violence and upheaval. I suspect, however, that radical change and authoritarian regimes will eventually emerge as part of our style in national politics. I find no reason to share your confidence in the survival of a liberal, capitalist system. Instead I find a compelling need to resort to rational activism, or political planning, to alleviate the worst hardships that now lie ahead.

ELI GINZBERG. A little arithmetic will reveal that in the forty-five years since FDR came to power we have seen only six years of political activism. The first four came at the start of the New Deal and the last two when LBJ launched the Great Society. I do not endorse Andrew Hacker's view that we believe in inept government; but neither do I share Robert Lekachman's view that the momentum of economic crisis will drive government toward energetic planning and economic activism. To be sure, if the economy should seriously unwind and real income should fall, we will probably see a rising political turmoil. On that score, David Apter's pessimism appears to be realistic. But I do not feel that we should double our planning energies to contend with the threat of decline.

I believe that there is reason to maintain a liberal belief in the durability of our system; or to use different language, I can reason for a conservative skepticism regarding the inevitability of radical change. First, there is already extensive machinery in place if a vigorous President should need to use it. We do not know how to control it well, but we do not have to design it from scratch or persuade the Congress to enact it in new legislation. Second, I am anxious about harmful and unintended side effects when government moves into an activist mode of planning and regulation. It can really do harm while meaning only to repair trouble.

I do not assume that government is so inept that it can only exacerbate crisis conditions and polarize social tensions. Moreover, the multiple linkages within the public sector, or between it and private industry, are too complex to be systematically fouled up in a short period of time. An energetic President might find difficulty in mastering the machinery; but his administration will also find it difficult to disrupt the machinery systematically. I find this to be an optimistic conclusion.

WALTER GOLDSTEIN. Our predictions of future crisis diverge sharply
into two rival prescriptions for contemporary action. On the conservative side, it is classically assumed that private industry should be regulated by the free flow of market forces—even when there is no market,
as in the case of telecommunications—and government is thus seen as a
clumsy if not a threatening evil to economic liberty. On the liberal side,
it is assumed that giant unions and corporations will readily concede
some of their power and privileges to the public sector so that social harmony and a spirit of political moderation can be sustained. Vested interests will remain largely inviolate, it is presumed, while public officials
police the marketplace as gentle night watchmen and reallocate social
payments to the neediest cases.

There is a third point of view to be considered, even though it has
been largely disregarded in this discussion. Robert Dahl, an anti-Marx-
ist, once suggested that government decisions do not stem from a "ma-
jestic march of great majorities" but from the relentless appeasement of
powerful groups. Dahl had set out to demonstrate that the structure of
the American economy was pluralistic and flexible but his Marxist critics
remained unconvinced. They insisted that power and economic interest
are tightly concentrated and that the hierarchies of finance capital are
remarkably impervious to political control. This collectivist critique provides a third point of view; it stresses the impossibility of imposing any
realistic mode of planning on a capitalist economy.

Two contemporary examples are cited by the "power elite" theorists
in rejecting the liberal credo that economic planning can be mixed with
a conservative economy. The first, in New York City, concerns the
power of the banks to reverse the priorities declared by a mismanaged
but elected government. The bankers' demand to exercise a tight surveillance over municipal expenditures reflects the priority to be granted
to unearned income over community services. It would be easier to accept this priority if a *quid pro quo* were also agreed upon; namely, that
city officials should protect the class interest of millions of citizens and
depositors by representing them, collectively, on the board of directors
of the giant banks. This might stop the banks from red-lining slum
ghettos or from investing local deposits of funds with firms overseas.

A second example of "power elite" criticism seeks to debunk the New
Deal. The radical critics argue that corporate industry was temporarily

willing to lose in tactical skirmishes so that it could win its major battles. The loss of ground to the progressive legislation of the 1930s was wrongly construed as a concession on the part of private capital. No great redistribution of income or power flowed from the concessions of the 1930s. So the critics insist that corporate wealth was basically strengthened, not weakened, by Franklin Roosevelt's efforts to reform the economic system.

Business Values and Political Controls

WALTER GOLDSTEIN. The business values of our society reflect a historically lasting consensus. Political parties have not run at election time against big business or the banks, not even in New York City. But this does not mean that the political system will always remain immune to change. The debates between left-of-center planners and conservative executives have been conducted with tolerance and compromise. Neither side has had much to lose and neither was very angry. But they did not represent the entire spectrum of political disagreements about our present turmoil and future fears. Both sides believed that planning involved a marginal rather than a fundamental restructuring in the arrangements of our society.

This raises a difficult problem of definition. If planning does not cause some pain, as any real transfer of power must do, should we even use the term? It is obvious that for want of a definition of "planning," corporations are said to manage, agencies to regulate, and politicians to program. As a result, some get richer, some enlarge their market or their institutional prestige. These adjustments might lead to serious instances of power loss but they cannot be viewed, collectively, as a major transfer in the concentration of power. The American economy has not experienced revolution or upheaval. It has merely adjusted, rather imperfectly, to limited thrusts of industrial and social change.

That government planning could deflect monetary policy, collective bargaining procedures, or stock exchange transactions is not doubted. But that the United States has moved far down the road toward central planning, or that it is even likely to do so, is immediately open to question. If one looked at the distribution of economic power today through the eyes of the mayor or the governor of New York, the banks appear to be more influential, well informed, and decisive than the political apparatus of the legislature, the political parties, or the muddled electoral process. In fact, the only decisive planning to be seen, beyond the budgetary confusion in Washington, is that appearing in the formidable management of resources in the private sector. That exerts a considerable influence over the expectations of public life.

ROBERT LEKACHMAN. I agree that a distinction must be preserved between the instrumental sense of planning and the more political connotation of setting goals or transferring power. The management tools of planning are designed for specific tasks while the policy programs pursued by planners are more extensive in aim and effect. Put in another way, resource managers specialize in microeconomic operations, the collection of data or the deployment of financial incentives; while policy planners search for strategies to redistribute power or income, to boost growth or to curb inflation. Their policy goals are determined by political values rather than by engineering or productivity techniques.

Walter Goldstein has emphasized that planning, at a policy level, requires attention to radical change or political upheaval. I have suggested that the absence of a forceful Left in American politics has limited our attention to planning objectives. Debates today focus on enlarging guidelines or statutory instruments rather than nationalizing private industries. Insofar as this relieves us of the burdensome and coercive planning followed in Eastern Europe, or the stumbling stagflation practiced in Western Europe, this bias has worked to our profit. But it must be recalled that the politics of the AFL-CIO or the Democratic Party pose no leftist threat to the capitalist system. Moreover, so long as business attracts the best talents away from politics or government, while offering the promise of material and psychic satisfaction to a consumer society, the popular demand for planning—by elected officials—will remain muted.

But how should we judge the argument that an economy of complex and plural structures defies planning; or indeed the alternative, that business monopolies are so entrenched that public planning can never be effective? My position is that planning began piecemeal some years ago; that planning to date has been a mixed success and could not easily be abandoned; and that it will inevitably increase in scope as the crises in our economic system intensify.

Four or five points support my argument. First, the long-run indicators in the economy tend to point downward. Unemployment is likely to persist at an unacceptably high level and so will the pressures of monetary inflation. Living standards for the mass of the population no longer move upward each year. David Apter is unfortunately correct in foreseeing a decline of civility and stability in our politics if the life-styles of the middle class are further eroded. Second, we have not learned how to control the major instruments of the economy. The confusion over monetary and physical controls, regulatory constraints and incomes policy, has denied us the benefits of balanced but dynamic growth. We do not know how to factor out of this confusion the drive toward equal employment opportunities, the cleaning up of the environment, the protection of consumers' or workers' interests, and a thrust to raise overall standards of productivity.

Third, to pile on the agony, there are secular forces that we cannot deflect. The price of energy continues to increase; it will surely continue as fuel-supply curves fail to keep pace with the expanding demand schedules of an energy-intense economy. The ability of the United States and other nations to meet their oil import bills will be curtailed if instability in world trade develops in the chilling manner suggested in Raymond Vernon's paper. Economic protection, currency devaluations, and trade wars will provoke considerable dislocation. Moreover, the shortage of primary commodities—including food and oil—will become more critical and threatening to each national economy with the passing of the years.

I have argued that the Left is not an energetic actor in American politics and that the campaign against business influence or corporate profits does not appear as an ominous threat. But two points remain to be made about the future role of corporate business. The first is that its leaders have already begun to respond to the vision of future economic crises by changing their position on public planning. Henry Ford II, Robert Roosa, Jay Miller, Michael Blumenthal, and Felix Rohatyn have willingly cooperated with the planning activities undertaken by the federal government or by New York and Detroit at the municipal level. Their cooperation has been strongly applauded by the business press and the larger industrial firms.

My second point is that it is strongly in the interest of business to participate in planning ventures that are accepted today with an enthusiasm unknown in the 1960s. Both of the parties and the presidential candidates in the 1976 elections were strongly responsive to business needs and both disavowed extreme policy commitments. Mr. Ford turned aside the ideological reaction of Mr. Reagan, while Mr. Carter emphasized at every turn that employment and growth must depend upon the profit-seeking initiatives of private capital.

I suspect that the inevitable courses of planning will be pinned, as Wassily Leontief reminded us, to the economic demands of business rather than to the political theorizing of radicals. Corporate managers recognize that the alternative to voluntary, participatory planning will be a regime that is more harsh and unsympathetic to business interests. They are pragmatic enough to know that we cannot turn back the clock of political movement. In the middle of a severe, lasting crisis we cannot revert to the laissez-faire doctrines that were associated erroneously with a past age of growth. Corporate managers know, too, that a conservative society can best conserve its position by rationalizing its allocation of scarce resources and by compromising over the control of economic growth. In the absence of a forceful Left, they would rather join an efficient government of conservatives than watch an inept administration divide the nation into warring ideological camps.

The practical considerations inherent in stabilizing the system lead me toward my conclusion. It is not the altruism of business but the growing cooperation between public and private agencies of power that will promote the course of economic planning. I only hope that they do it well.

THE POLITICS OF PLANNING
FOR THE PUBLIC INTEREST

The Role of Liberal Ideology
in a Conservative Society

WALTER GOLDSTEIN

POLITICAL IDEOLOGY has been remarkably constrained for 200 years
and remarkably inconsistent with American economic behavior. "Big"
government and official intervention in the marketplace have been re-
lentlessly opposed but regularly extended. Madison's belief, that "the
best government is that which governs least," was widely extolled and
also ignored. In the formative as in the mature eras of American capitalism, it was often the entrepreneurs and the owners of capital who
pressed for collectivist benefits. Ideology notwithstanding, they lobbied for an increase in interstate controls, in protectionist tariffs, or in
monetary restraints. Their professed aim was not to inhibit but to stabilize the business environment. Today we find a greater contradiction between the political belief in a laissez-faire market and the

Walter Goldstein is professor of political science at the State University of New York at
Albany and chairman of the University Seminar on Technology and Social Change at
Columbia.

expectation that economic activity must be controlled. We continue to conjure up the imagery of an open market in the political and economic systems, as if they operated independently of each other, but we increasingly resort to closure practices to fine-tune both of them simultaneously.

Since the early days of the republic, when Jefferson and Hamilton first argued over the trading privileges to be granted to aggressive entrepreneurs, the confusion has continued to escalate. Popular folklore held that the business of a free country was indeed business. But it was the captains of industry who sought one infringement of the principle after another. As the product worth of the American economy grew beyond $1,000 billion a year, and as its leading corporate units achieved astronomical sales and growth, the confusion became more intense. Public-interest groups began to clamor for antitrust legislation, environmental safeguards, and fiscal constraints. In response, opposition mounted among the business community and among conservative economists. They protested not so much on principle but because of the particular sets of taxes, statutes, or legislative curbs that had been adopted.[1]

The political conflict between business expectations and government regulations is longer-lived than contemporary critics tend to recall. The myth was generated in the last century that the dynamic growth of the U.S. economy should be attributed to the genius of merchant tycoons, statesman bankers, and risk-taking visionaries. Although the impact of an Andrew Carnegie or a John D. Rockefeller must not be underestimated, nor should the demands that they made to enlarge government services and protection. Given the pioneering élan of nineteenth-century capitalism, they were almost as convinced as Presidents Nixon and Ford that a benign collectivism was indispensable to the survival of a market economy.

The confusion of political debate reaches deeply into the American economy and its role in world affairs. As an exemplar of "free world capitalism" the United States has not only traded profitably with the socialist economies but it also has begun to imitate their domestic economic

---

[1] An excellent analysis of the political struggles both within and between the Republican and Democratic parties appears in Otis L. Graham, Jr., *Toward a Planned Society* (New York: Oxford Univ. Press, 1976); he contrasts the partial maneuvers as against the full-blown rhetoric that propelled U.S. politics between the administrations of FDR and Nixon–Ford.

practices. Our defense and aerospace industries have come to rely almost exclusively on public funds; the monetary and banking sectors are rigorously controlled; and giant multinational enterprises have begun to compete in complexity with the bureaucratic monoliths that dominate the communist hierarchy of planning empires. Secure from the economic risk and the capital uncertainties that should be found in a competitive market, our giant corporations rely on public planning agencies to stabilize (or subsidize) an environment of oligopoly equilibrium. It was in their corporate interest that the subventions and regulatory constraints of government should be better ordered and enlarged. Their only complaint today, as the oil companies put it, is that public policy has been neither flexible nor selective enough to satisfy their needs.[2]

Ignoring their own rhetoric against big government, conservative and liberal administrations alike have maintained federal outlays at the constant level of 20 percent of GNP and federal employment at 3 percent of the work force. The ratios shifted slightly up or down in the thirty years since World War II, usually in line with prevailing rates of inflation or unemployment, but the absolute dimensions increased as the GNP and the population continued to expand.[3] Conservatives called for "less government" and more freedom for business but it was the Republicans in Washington who ran up record deficits and who added each year to the national debt. The liberals were accused (often correctly) of trying to solve social and economic difficulties by "throwing money at problems." But their conservative opponents, while opposing the "lavish spending" of the New Deal and the Great Society, were also committed to the financing of vast government programs to support the economy.[4]

[2] The reliance by corporate managers upon government agencies and regulations to subsidize defense industries, to stabilize oligopolies, and to promote monetary policy is the central theme of Edward S. Greenberg, *Serving the Few: Corporate Capitalism and the Bias of Government Policy* (New York: Wiley, 1974).

[3] It should be noted that government payrolls have doubled in the last twenty years; with 3 million persons employed at the federal level and 12 million at the state and local levels, government accounts for one-fifth of the total work force. In the ten years between 1965 and 1975, state and local expenditures rose from $101 to $318.5 billion.

[4] That government will intervene vigorously in financial policy is now a basic expectation of business interests and of bipartisan politics. For a multiple set of interventionist expectations see Michael H. Best and William E. Connolly, *The Politicized Economy* (Lexington, Mass.: D. C. Heath, 1976), and Robert L. Heilbroner, "The American Plan," *New York Times Magazine*, 27 January 1975.

The Changing Economy

Important changes have occurred in the last thirty years and their repercussions remain the basic source of partisan debate. State and local government expenditures and payrolls have tripled, moving from 5 toward 15 percent of both GNP and the work force. This reflected the social consensus that educational welfare benefits must rise as the baby boom brought a 40 percent increase in the population. Today total outlays (federal, state, and local) account for 35 percent of GNP. Rather than reduce these public outlays, the Republican administrations of 1968–1976 utilized them to cope with the inflation and recession that followed the Vietnam war. On frequent occasions the Republicans repudiated business doctrine by intervening in credit markets, by inflating the money supply or by regulating consumer prices. Their activism was regretted by only the most conservative factions; they viewed the Federal Reserve System and its redoubtable chairman, Arthur Burns, not as a stalwart defender but as an ominous opponent of free enterprise.[5]

Another important change resulted in a bipartisan adoption of antibusiness values, and a wider belief in government spending and planning programs. The business of America changed as the work force shifted out of agriculture and into service sector employment. The change was facilitated by the provision of extensive tax credits, government procurements, labor legislation, and costly building programs. A suburban location for new housing and industry was encouraged by tax shelter inducements. By contrast, manufacturing employment in the blue-collar industries declined as the older cities of the Northeast and Midwest fell into disrepair. The center cities were left helpless in the face of racial conflict, inadequate financing, and housing dilapidation; while new industries, with value added by government procurements,

---

[5] The business uses of reflationary policy reflect the uneven access to power and the inequitable distribution of wealth that had survived three generations of tax, welfare, and transfer-payment programs. In 1952 transfer payments amounted to 5.5 percent of diposable income; in 1972 they were 16 percent. Yet in 1972 the top 5 percent of U.S. families received 15.9 percent of aggregate income and the top 20 percent took 41.4 percent (a mere 2 percent less than 25 years before). Moreover, 0.5 percent of the adult population controlled 33 percent of private wealth in 1972, and the wealthiest 2 percent held two-thirds of all corporate stock; with bonds, mortgages, and other income included, 20 percent own 77 percent of all private wealth. Even if one-sixth (16 percent) of personal income is now transferred outside the work-incentive economy, it is evident that great inequalities are durably built into our society.

moved skilled work from the older urban centers to the swiftly growing cities of the South and West.[6]

It is true that government intervention did help generate one remarkable success. The supply of jobs increased in numbers as the population grew and as the percentage of working women rose (from 18 to almost 40 percent). But even this increase, to 90 million jobs, was not sufficient to absorb the baby boom of the postwar years. It is now estimated that unemployment might remain permanently stuck between 6 and 8 percent (but at 40 percent for inner-city and minority youth), thus producing a generation of permanently damaged graduates of the welfare system. Although annual spending on welfare rose beyond $150 billion a year, this served only to cushion the market economy but not to stimulate activity to the level of economic and human utilization that was desired.[7] The failure of planners to train and to provide better opportunities for a skilled work force is now becoming painfully clear. That the planners lack political authority, rather than technical proficiency, is also apparent. It is obviously unjust to blame the manpower economists for miscalculating employment schedules when the schedules are determined by corporate managers who must, themselves, gamble with risk capital in order to create jobs.

The change from a manufacturing to a service sector emphasis in our "postindustrial economy" has brought a further set of political difficulties. Contemporary society depends on rapid changes in industrial technology, an educated work force, regulated utilities, expensive welfare-delivery systems, and a rapid growth of GNP. Ironically, our belief in a limited, night watchman state has been more resilient in theory than in practice.[8] Although rhetoric pretends that an invisible hand runs the machinery of the market, in practice excellent skills in

[6] Inducements to encourage the running down of inner cities, older housing, and labor-intensive industries are noted in Robert Lekachman, *Economists at Bay: Why the Experts Will Never Solve Your Problems* (New York: McGraw-Hill, 1976), pp. 134–38.

[7] The importance of welfare payments to alleviate the worst social defects of a market economy are analyzed in detail in the numerous manpower studies of Eli Ginzberg: his latest is *The Human Economy* (New York: McGraw-Hill, 1976).

[8] The shift of employment from agricultural and manufacturing to service sector industries is noted in a critical appraisal of the "postindustrial society" by Robert L. Heilbroner, *Business Civilization in Decline* (New York: Norton, 1976), pp. 63–69. Professors Ginzberg, Heilbroner, and Lekachman are long-standing members of the Seminar on Technology and Social Change at Columbia University, which cosponsored this book and conference.

lobbying have been developed by corporations, such as ITT or Gulf, that sought additional political power or economic subventions.

One can cite a key example of the new conservatism of the 1970s. Mr. Nixon insisted upon doubling the size of the White House staff so that he could centralize his grasp of the new agencies and departments that he had built into the Washington power structure. That he misused his control apparatus is of less significance, in the long run, than his achievement in carrying the federal budget (with huge, inflationary deficits) to $450 billion a year.[9] He won enormous campaign contributions from big business in 1972 to curb the power of big government but his economic policies reversed all of his rhetorical commitments. Until the Watergate dam broke, many of his business supporters praised him for his clever reversals and his flexible policies.

It is striking that the political rhetoric of the 1970s still intones the fears expressed in 1944 by Frederick von Hayek in *The Road to Serfdom*. Statist power is everywhere to be distrusted though, apparently, it is everywhere to be enlarged. As ideologists of private enterprise, the energies of the Treasury Secretaries, such as Connally and Simon, were no less interventionist than those of the Great Society and the Kennedy idealists whom they had replaced. Once their entrepreneurial beliefs were put aside, the Republican leaders and their business colleagues moved to expand the food stamp program, federal revenue-sharing, environmental protection constraints, Social Security benefits, Medicare, unemployment assistance, the subsidizing of rail and road transportation, the regulation of energy industries, and the enlargement of industrial safety controls. Instead of turning back the clock of change, they added to the prestige and the authority of public sector involvements.[10]

This spirit of pragmatism, though it ran counter to previous fears of central planning, began to raise new demands for public programs

[9] The impressive record of enlarging government bureaucracies, deficits, and regulations is detailed in Otis Graham, *Toward a Planned Society*. He recalls (pp. 260–261) Walter Lippmann's comment in 1935 that "radical transitions in a nation's life are best carried through by conservative men," and he adds the criticism voiced by a key Nixon appointee: "At the White House we had often talked about long-range planning but we rarely did it—we were almost entirely crisis oriented."

[10] The business support for and the political mileage gained by the Congress in its role as a corporate lobbyist is elaborated in Ira Katznelson and Mark Kesselman, *The Politics of Power* (New York: Harcourt, 1975), and in Martin Tolchin and Susan Tochin, *To the Victors* (New York: Vintage, 1971).

among conservative businessmen. A prime example appeared in Roy Ash, the director of the Office of Management and Budget and a key member of the White House staff. As a dedicated capitalist who had built a once-profitable conglomerate (Litton Industries) on a pyramid of defense contracts and takeover maneuvers, Ash was responsible for the reorganizing and the better managing of the federal bureaucracy. He personified the accomplishments that businessmen could realize by improving rather than reducing the capabilities of government planning.[11]

Another representative of the conservative, managerial elite was Daniel Patrick Moynihan. He articulated the antiplanning arguments of his Harvard colleagues in *The Public Interest*. He rejected money-spending liberalism, and he shared the distrust of government activism that appeared in Edward Banfield's attack, in *The Unheavenly City*, against "the reign of error."[12] Yet it was his task, as Nixon's director of the Domestic Council, to restructure the multiple welfare programs and the hydra-headed agencies working with HEW, HUD, DOT, OEO, and other high-spending departments.

A third leader, not to be overlooked, was Nelson Rockefeller. With family holdings in Exxon, the Chase Manhattan Bank, and a dozen multinational interests, Rockefeller extended the responsibilities of the State of New York in a reckless mode of *étatisme*. He brought the state to virtual bankruptcy before ending his fifteen years as governor to return to the Washington power structure. His combination of business rhetoric and government activism enraged a major faction in his own party; in expanding the authority and the financial burden of the public sector, he was seen as a traitor to his class.[13]

[11] The large staff recruited by Roy Ash to implement the centralized controls of the Domestic Council and OMB drew the angry response from a conservative congressman that this was "the most far-reaching reorganization of the executive branch that has ever been proposed by a president of the United States"; Otis Graham, *Toward a Planned Society*, p. 206.

[12] As a prominently liberal conservative on the Harvard faculty, Moynihan was given the responsibility for improving (not abolishing) the 435 model cities, OEO, and welfare planning programs that had been inherited from LBJ's cornucopia, the Great Society. He worked closely with John Ehrlichman, a member of the American Institute of Planners who had once specialized in zoning law and who helped Nixon launch a great range of muncipal and welfare financing plans.

[13] Rockefeller had first led a study of organization in the executive branch in the 1950s, and he continued his efforts in the Rockefeller Brothers' report of 1959 and the Commis-

The sophisticated exercises in planning performed in the private sector have also influenced the debate over economic planning. Corporate giants such as AT&T or IBM have recruited large planning staffs. Furthermore, the capability of planners employed by universities, foundations, cities, and the military is now too well known to be disregarded. It is difficult to reject planning on ideological grounds when the investment projections, the systems analyses, and the production schedules of major corporations can generate a phenomenal rate of growth. In short, if planning helps boost the profits realized through industrial concentrations, it must be recognized by business theorists as a social virtue.[14]

It is clearly illogical to reject our reliance on complex planning capaclose to $50 billion in sales each year. This exceeds the sum of the general revenues levied by the six states of New England, plus New York, New Jersey, and Pennsylvania. Employing nearly 750,000 workers in 127 plants in the United States and 45 overseas, GM pays wages equal to twice the personal income of Ireland, and it pays dividends to a population larger than that of Washington, D.C. It should be added that GM is just one of the successful entities among the 227 corporations whose sales exceed $1 billion a year and just one of the 36 giants whose turnover exceeds $5 billion a year. Considering its intimate relations with the public sector, it is difficult to cite GM and its like as a convincing cause to curb future planning programs.[15]

sion on Critical Choices in 1974. The vast expenditures and bureaucracies that he launched as governor of New York are appraised in successive issues of a policy journal, *Empire State Report,* between 1975 and 1977.

[14] Annual figures on industrial concentration appear each May in *Fortune* magazine. In 1977 the top 500 firms accounted for $971 billion in sales and $49.4 billion in profits; 36 companies exceeded $5 billion each in sales and 227 exceeded $1 billion. The top 15 banks held more than $10 billion each in assets, many of them more than $35 billion. Looking at just the *four* largest firms in each industry: they accounted for 99 percent of automobile production, 96 percent of aluminum fabrication, 80 percent of cigarette output, 72 percent of soaps and detergent, and more than 60 percent of many more sectors. The top 500 recorded two-thirds of all manufacturing sales and three-fourths of manufacturing employment. Soviet ideologues might well envy such a planning record.

[15] The data on General Motors originally appeared in Richard J. Barber, *The American Corporation* (New York: Dutton, 1970), p. 20. In 1977 GM's turnover was $47 billion, its net income was $2.9 billion, its employees numbered 780,000, and its total return to investors (dividend yield plus price appreciation) was 45.8 percent. Among the nonmanufacturing giants, AT&T held assets of $87 billion, its revenues were $33 billion, its net income was $3.8 billion, and it employed 927,000 persons. These figures suggest the scale and the success of economic planning in the private sector.

Planning and Ideology

It appears, therefore, that the debate over planning concerns the ideological thrust rather than the economic scale of a market-oriented society. Planning for profit and growth is widely praised; so, too, are the operations of government that help stabilize the monetary supply, oligopoly equilibrium, or the reflation of the economy. Business and labor interests urge the Federal Reserve Bank, the Department of Commerce or HEW, or the regulatory agencies (such as the CAB, the FTC, the ICC, or the FCC) to change their rulings but not to abandon them. Each industry complains about the award of franchises, subventions, tax credits, or procurements in its specific market but not about the general necessity for government intervention, per se. This selectivity tends to undermine the ideological defense of private enterprise and to blunt the protest against collective planning.[16]

A similar point is made in each of the preceding papers in this volume. Andrew Hacker notes that the American people, their political rhetoric notwithstanding, have come to expect more not less intervention by government agencies. Although skeptical about the quality of the government's information and intervention, Eli Ginzberg details the vital role that it plays in regulating welfare support and manpower policy. A similar theme appears in Raymond Vernon's analysis of international trade and foreign investment; like every other regime, the U.S. government is required to manipulate trading currencies in its attempts to balance external payments. Franklin Long extends the point in weighing the performance of civil and military agencies which allocate public expenditures and support priorities for the nation's R&D efforts.[17]

[16] The need for full-scale collaboration between business and government to rationalize economic growth rates and business allocations is stated by Thornton Bradshaw, the president of the Atlantic Richfield Oil Co., in "My Case for National Planning," *Fortune*, February 1977; a rejoinder appeared in the March issue, "The Deceptive Allure of National Planning" by Tom Alexander.

[17] Three indicators of federal regulation were cited in a special feature on "Government Intervention," in *Business Week*, April 4, 1977: between 1970 and 1975, economic regulatory agencies increased their budgets from $166 million to $428 million a year; social agencies increased their spending from $1.4 billion to $4.3 billion; and the *Code of Federal Regulations* grew from 54,105 to 72,200 pages. Murray Weidenbaum added that the cost to industry of compiling forms and complying with the flow of regulations was highly burdensome; in some cases, it cost a large company $150 million a year.

The disagreement over the costs and benefits of public planning appears in the rival positions taken by Murray Weidenbaum and Robert Lekachman. The first insists that the costly and proliferating encroachments of government regulation have succeeded, more massively than we generally admit, in inhibiting the entrepreneurial dynamic and the productive growth of the U.S. economy. The latter argues that our economy is overextended and that it lacks a serious capability for policy forecasting and coordination; hence it is widely believed that planning will become an "inevitable necessity." The political problem, as Lekachman puts it, is that we cannot afford to admit that the time for serious planning has now come. There are too many groups who hesitate to accept the political consequences of such an admission.

The case argued by the AT&T executives in these pages is in no way inconsistent with the contemporary debate in American society. The managers of the Bell System tend to agree with Weidenbaum on general principles but to sympathize with Lekachman's views in seeking a better regulation of their own interests. They oppose the political extension of regulation on ideological grounds, but they recognize the need for more thorough planning in their own industry. This division in corporate thinking is to be found in many industries. Airlines, truckers, utilities, banks, insurance, and manufacturing companies all seek more sensitive modes of regulatory protection in their own sector—but less government interference in all others.[18]

The identification of the public interest has been confused in recent years by the scramble for political power, corporate profit, and sector maneuver among loudly contesting groups. It has been assumed that the "public interest" is simply the residue of aggregate group demands. As a result, oligopoly competition in the basic industries of the economy has become politically acceptable and economically entrenched. Drawing large campaign contributions from the big four (or six or eight) companies in aerospace, oil, pharmaceutical, or electronics industries, both political parties have bent the powers of government to promote the interests of these critical power blocs in the economy.[19]

[18] The determination of the airline, trucking, banking, insurance, and telecommunications industries to stave off deregulation or antitrust actions has been extensively chronicled. See Paul H. Weaver, "Unlocking the Gilded Cage of Regulation," *Fortune*, February 1977, and Ralph Nader et al., *Taming the Giant Corporation* (New York: Norton, 1976).

[19] The extensive business contributions to CREEP in the 1972 reelection of Nixon, and in previous years for other candidates, were revealed in the Watergate hearings. A large

Organized labor has sought an equally powerful leverage, either through channeling campaign contributions to certain candidates or through expensive lobbying efforts in the federal or state legislatures. It was assumed in the expansionist days that preceded the onset of inflation and recession (in the 1970s) that the public interest would best be served by an orderly clash of big business, labor, and government. As a triad of power holders they were supposed to manage the national economy, plan its future growth, and distribute its ever growing dividends.[20]

The political bargaining built into the planning process in the 1950s and 1960s was perceived as the spin-off benefit needed to sustain a pluralist political system. Support for this belief was drawn from the experience that was perceived in other industrial economies. Japan and Germany had achieved a social quietism together with unprecedented rates of growth; their success, it was assumed, derived from the political sensitivity with which the powers of government had been mobilized on behalf of the key institutions in the private sector. Less confidence was drawn from the indicative planning practiced in France and to a different extent in Sweden. By contrast, the failure of central planning and nationalization in Britain was supposed to demonstrate the folly of conceding excessive powers to the public sector.[21]

These comforting conclusions were demolished in the 1970s as the inflationary consequences of the Vietnam war, mixed with a 500 percent hike in the price of oil, brought havoc to many of the advanced industrial economies. It became apparent that the pluralist trade-offs, the

---

number of companies were obliged to fire senior executives and to apologize to shareholders. In most cases the largest contributions, to political parties in the United States or overseas, came from oligopoly interests. Presumably they found a good business return in spending millions of dollars to win political influence.

[20] The original theory of a triadic equilibrium of forces appeared in J. K. Galbraith's *American Capitalism* in 1952 (Boston, Houghton). In his later work, such as *The New Industrial State* (Boston: Houghton, 1967) and *Economics and the Public Purpose* (Boston: Houghton, 1973), Galbraith came to view this equilibrium as a reprehensible restraint on competitive trade and consumer sovereignty. Lekachman noted, in *Economists at Bay*, pp. 141–46, that many industries contributed to the thrust of stagflation in 1974 by continuing to raise prices while their sales volume declined, thus negating a cardinal expectation of competitive market behavior.

[21] A useful analysis of the gains and failures of planning exercises overseas appears in Jack Hayward and Michael Watson, eds., *Planning, Politics and Public Policy: The British, French and Italian Experience* (New York: Cambridge Univ. Press, 1975); and in Raymond Vernon, *Storm over the Multinationals: The Real Issues* (Cambridge: Harvard Univ. Press, 1977).

group power struggles, the triad concentration of political influence, and
the two party stand-off could no longer guarantee the fullest use of social
and economic resources. Stagflation settled in as a permanent, structural
characteristic of Western life. Nation-states became more protectionist
as their energy problems multiplied and as their balance of payments
deteriorated. The pluralist bargains and compromises between economic
groups eroded as greater demands were made on the distributive mechanisms of the capitalist state. Oligopoly industry and labor organizations
sought public protection against the threat of inflation, recession, and
foreign competition by lobbying for subventions at home and trade-war
maneuvers abroad. The lowest common multiple of factional gain, once
known as the public interest, was fragmented by the internal divisions
and the external struggles of powerful sectoral groups.

A new concept emerged in the resulting chaos: the Brokerage State.
As the Democrats replaced the post-Watergate administration of the
Republican party, in 1977, the bipartisan consensus was once again re-
newed. The U.S. economy had to be revived and expanded by a judi-
cious mix of fiscal stimuli, credit management, protective trade policies,
welfare subsidies, and industrial regulation. The rhetoric of liberalism
and conservatism regained its customary irrelevance after the presidential election maneuvers had been completed. The liberals pressed, in
vain, for the deregulation of oligopoly industry and the conservatives (in
both parties) restored the protective benefits that industry expected as
its rightful due from government. Invoking their ancient belief in consumer sovereignty, both parties utilized power to safeguard producers'
interests and to still the perturbations threatened by competitive trading
and pricing initiatives.

New twists in the debate over collective planning emerged as the
U.S. economy recovered from the 1974–1976 recession. First, the liberals claimed that the Brokerage State had been poorly managed and
that better forecasting capabilities must be created by capitalist interests. At the same time they argued that the state had looked after the
needs of noncompetitive industry but not the marginal demands of consumers, wage earners, and organized workers. Their general concern
seemed to focus on oligopoly mismanagement rather than on the traditional, liberal appeal for social justice.[22]

[22] The Trilateral Commission brought together a prestigious group of corporate, labor,
and media executives to issue a new report on the need to stabilize the "liberal" economy

As a second development, there was a sharpening of conservative interest in the mercantilist successes of "Japan Inc." and the European Economic Community. It became respectable to advocate a comparable collaboration of big industry and big government. "State capitalism" or business-minded government was recommended for the U.S. economy as a model to revive the nation's energies and structures. Global oil companies, the Pentagon bureaucracy, and the UAW were urged to start management enrichment programs; they would then be able to better coordinate the nation's resources and its policy forecasting technologies. Decision processes in the public and private sector should be systematically brought together, not forced apart. Differences might be expressed regarding the optimum "mix" of public or private planning capabilities, but no one argued the case for either political confrontation or radical change.

Third, liberals agreed to the notion that industrial concentration was passably efficient though not particularly democratic. Conservatives resigned themselves to the continuing expansion of public sector payments and regulations in the expectation that these instruments could stabilize an oligopoly market. In fact, both were profoundly wrong.[23]

Realignment Without Redistribution

The new consensus about planning stemmed from a long-lived, historic misunderstanding. The debate between liberal and conservative strategists had been conducted within strictly confined parameters. With no forceful Left to prod them toward socialism, the liberals have settled for marginal adjustments rather than fundamental changes in the distribution of economic power. Most of them gauged the planning functions of the Brokerage State in terms of its instrumental performance.

and to regain the confidence of the consumer-electorate: *The Crisis of Democracy* (New York: New York Univ. Press, 1975). The group's anxiety was moved by then-current public opinion polls; they showed a 26 percent fall-off in confidence in the major companies (from 55 percent in 1966 to 29 percent in 1973) and a remarkable increase (from 18 percent in 1958 to 53 percent in 1972) of those who believed that the government "is pretty much run by a few big interests."

[23] In a survey prior to the 1976 election an editorial in *Fortune*, "The Economics of the Candidates" (October 1976), rebuked both political parties for supporting a highly interventionist set of policies. Carter had expressed his concern at the inefficiency of the bureaucracy and Ford at its economic cost, but both had failed to rally the country to a firm protest against further extensions of government regulation and direction.

Following the pragmatic compromises of FDR and the New Deal, they chose to maintain the conventional distributions of unearned income, tax shelters, political subsidies, union bargaining, and industrial concentration. They resisted, by and large, the need to break up oligopolies, to eradicate inequalities in income and privilege, or to extend the collective planning authority of the state. The mainstream of liberalism believed in the orderly management of pluralist compromise and pragmatic moderation in allocating the benefits drawn from a growing economy. Rejecting the 1972 "excesses" in the campaign platform adopted by George McGovern, liberal leaders and the AFL-CIO repudiated the cause of levelers, populists, democratic socialists, or anti-business critics. President Carter reflected these commitments in his choice of Cabinet appointments and market-sensitive programs.[24]

Conservative interests in American society were no less committed to the cause of compromise. They accepted the manipulative and interventionist instruments of Keynesian policy with only passing demurrals. Instead of scheming for a return to the halcyon modes of private enterprise, they continued to enlarge the regulatory agencies and the bureaucratic expenditures of central government. Some of them dissented by clamoring against the inflationary consequences of welfare spending, the inhibitory burden of government planning, and the unjust taxation imposed on higher-income groups. But the conservatives in the mainstream refused to eliminate the minimum wage laws, the progressive tax schedules, and the environmental controls that the hard-line enthusiasts had sought. The financial deficits incurred through massive welfare (plus defense) programs were not cut; they were increased. The power of organized labor was left largely intact. The collaboration between public and private planning agencies was greatly extended; and corporate managers moved with increasing frequency to assume executive responsibilities in regulatory agencies. In short, the conservatives rejected the doctrine of laissez-faire as forcefully as the liberals had forsaken the appeal for collectivist policies.[25]

[24] The economic policies and the cabinet appointments of the Carter administration were subjected to a stronger attack by labor than by business interests. Once the proposed tax rebates and other egalitarian measures were abandoned, conservative forces in early 1977 were less critical than liberal Democrats or the AFL-CIO.

[25] The charge is frequently made that regulated interests have "captured" the regulators, and that antitrust injunctions have not been pushed with dispatch lest they harm the in-

The unreality of the ideological dispute over economic planning can be seen today in the tacit consensus that dominates the political center of American life. It appears that most liberals and conservatives have rejected the cause of radical change. Neither challenges the prevailing structure of property relations, the economic jurisdiction of corporate wealth, or the skewed distribution of fiscal rewards. Both sides are content in practice, if not in theory, with the pragmatic compromises of a dual or "mixed" economy. The liberals do not aim to build the cluster of central mechanisms that would be needed to implement collectivist planning or redistributive policy commitments. The conservatives have rejected any attempt to dismember the administrative apparatus of big government. But both have also revealed their inability to cope with the fundamental and structural problems of the economy. As a result of their impasse, the persistent thrusts of inflation and unemployment have blocked many future courses for economic growth.[26]

It appears that there is a bipartisan agreement in contemporary debate to restrict the issues exclusively to technical and instrumental concerns. Improving the coordination of policy mechanisms, either within the corporate or the state-run sectors, is the function that absorbs the attention of economists, party strategists, and policy managers. Planning "by whom" is the critical question, not "for whom." It is assumed that the problems of poverty, inequality, and racism are not particularly salient. It is also assumed that social constituencies will remain basically stable, and that the fragmenting of underemployed families in the decaying cities will not disrupt the status quo. The emergence of new factions, such as consumer groups, welfare associations, or break-away labor organizations, suggests that these assumptions may no longer be tenable.

---

dustries under investigation. In fact, just two cases could use all the limited staff and investigative capabilities of the Justice Department: IBM and AT&T. Together their earnings are nearly $50 billion or 3 percent of GNP. They employ hundreds of skilled lawyers and they expect to drag out litigation for the next ten years (*Business Week*, October 4, 1976), thus exhausting the watchdogs who are supposed to police them.

[26] Thurman Arnold condemned the noise rather than the reality of government threats in *The Folklore of American Capitalism* (New Haven: Yale Univ. Press, 1937). He argued (p. 212) that "the actual result of the anti-trust laws was to promote the growth of industrial organizations by deflecting the attack on them into purely moral and ceremonial channels." His case has not changed in forty years.

In this regard, there has been a marked rise in nonparty or "independent" registrations among voters and a steep fall in the respect paid toward industrial corporations. Public opinion polls indicate the similarly poor esteem in which other institutions are held, including the President, the Congress, the military, and the press. Nowhere is the fall more evident than in city politics. As the delivery of services declined and financial solvency eroded, the political coalitions that once ruled urban politics and the corporate economy began to disintegrate. Municipal planning functions were undermined on the one side by political alienation and on the other by corporate flight. It was the failure of bipartisan policies at the grass-roots level, rather than the polarizing of group struggles at a national level, that broke apart the social infrastructure of New York and other cities. Private planning led to the redlining of entire neighborhoods by the banks and to the termination of employment by runaway firms. No countervailing power was provided for municipal planners to arrest the course of urban decay.[27]

Conclusion

The confusion of authority in American society points today toward an important conclusion. The pluralist politics of the past no longer work reliably and cannot cope with the slowing down of economic growth. Unfortunately, the clinging to outworn doctrine is so pervasive that it has obscured our need to improve methods of economic forecasting, systems planning, and resource allocation. Irresponsible and layered bureaucracies, whether in the HEW or in the anonymous echelons of the commercial banks, have impeded the development of new planning devices; they have also ignored the changing needs of their client constituencies. As a consequence, private firms or local governments have increased their expenditures and their service activities but not their efficiency or their clients' involvement. Driven by the pressures of stagfla-

---

[27] The "opportunity" gains of the urban middle class have appeared in school subsidies, business allowances, and home-owner deductions. These have often been paid by the "opportunity" costs of the underprivileged, the unskilled, or home-renting citizens. The advantages offered by a state-run university or by the pension schemes of the state civil service are not shared by the inner-city blacks or by millions of unemployed teenagers; their subventions appear in less secure and more controversial modes of welfare transfers.

tion, industrial, retail, and labor interests have struggled to protect themselves from commercial competition, from public enquiry, or from political accountability. In many cases, the political lobbying of energy, utility, or manufacturing firms has disregarded the claims of their customers and critics, or of the nation at large.

A residual expression of the public interest has been voiced, with scant success, by maverick voters, consumers, or public-policy groups. Their numbers are small, however, and they can not match the expert knowledge held by multinational firms, investment banks, public bureaucracies, network media, or national labor unions. They do not know how to combat Establishment task forces, professional lobbyists, or elite pretenses to simulate participatory public planning and policy control. As the pieties of the Bicentennial celebrations faded away, it became evident that the market system of distributing political and economic power had performed in a remarkably poor manner. But it also appeared that the energy needed to revitalize their operations had simply run out. The vision needed to conceive of new principles and alternative designs to order a postindustrial civilization were no longer of public concern.

In previous depressions it was believed that a key function of government was the repair of structural and distributive defects in the market economy. This belief has largely evaporated. Today it is assumed that the need for policy change can be gauged with some accuracy from changes in the modal distribution of purchasing power. Under this formula the Federal Reserve System is supposed to plan the monetary needs of the economy; it is trusted by business while the elected President and Congress are not. If the Fed chooses to hike interest rates or to fear inflation more than unemployment, its appointive officers can massage and financially deflect market forces. Thus railroads, medical centers, or energy utilities can find new financing so long as they can reasonably earn a return on their equity. If purchasing power and profit margins are inadequate, as in urban transit or housing or education, social transfer payments and policy choices must be regarded not as hard investments but as charitable bequests from soft funding. In this manner we bias the definition of what is necessary or indispensable to the public good. We invest for profit but we endow social causes with guilt.

Two factors distinguish our present predicatment. The first is the remarkable absence of political anger or social polarization. After a rich in-

take of pluralist politics and Keynesian economics, the political system
has learned to live with the indigestible problems of urban poverty,
racial discrimination, and social injustice. As R. H. Tawney once suggested, an affluent society is cursed into a false belief: that each consumer
will satisfy the demands of social greed by promoting his own acquisi-
tiveness. This prophecy was not believed twenty years ago but it is today.
The poor and the unemployed do not storm the glass skyscrapers of Ci-
tibank, G.M., the UAW, or the U.S. Department of the Treasury. It is
evident that we have lost interest in revolutionary change. But it is foolish
to suppose that the interlocking power arrangements and the institutional
compromises of our society will survive for years without end.

A second factor appears in our emotional insistence that the economy
will weather the storms of the future as easily as it did in the past. Little
attention is paid to the probability that cheap energy, plentiful jobs,
equity capital, and corporate wisdom might become scarce commodities.
Nor do we unduly concern ourselves over the likelihood that our
cities, schools, housing, and welfare services will fall into bankruptcy
and decay. It is argued that we survived previous crises without resorting to indicative planning, systems forecasts, anticipatory allocations, an
incomes policy, price controls, bureaucratic reforms, or a realignment of
public and private interest configurations. It is now asserted that we can
master future difficulties by clinging to traditional beliefs and practices.
A rude shock might come when we discover the costs of this error. The
shock might first appear as a threat to ration gasoline, to rationalize labor
practices, or to allocate scarce investment funds among key industries.
Should it materialize, the shock will expose (possibly in an abrupt manner)
the unyielding obsolescence in our cultural expectations and the idiocy of
our belief in timeless historical growth.

It is often said that American political life is guided not by logic but by
two centuries of economic pragmatism. This has prompted us to create
sophisticated instruments for long-range forecasting and budget balancing but to confine them within the foundations of outmoded belief. We
have argued that folklore demands to optimize profit and to preserve the
settled social order are compatible with an electronic, data-based system
of government. Industrial, labor, and political leaders have insisted that
any political thrust for reform must remain at all times within the
bounds of orthodoxy. In short, that it would be offensive and polit-

ically alien to finance full employment by altering the rules of group bargaining or by relying too heavily on fallible institutions outside the market. Conventional wisdom dictates that the system should not be subjected to abrupt change or coercive reform. Although they are well enough armed with data to sustain their own skepticism, both liberals and conservatives are quick to agree to this article of faith. As a result, the debate over planning remains blind to the pressing changes of time and deaf to the protests of the disenfranchised.

It is not tenable to conclude that the system will retain its planless equilibrium for an indefinite future, or that it will successfully cope with future threats within the parameters of past experience. There is reason to question whether the system is still flexible enough to change, and to ask whether a settled society can summon any idealism or determination to renew its economic vigor. So long as the function of planning is conceived in a narrow gauge and technocratic mode, the answer to these questions will probably be negative.

By definition, economic planning and systems forecasting must cope with the broadest questions of social redistribution and political change. The engineering skills provided at the present time of stress, whether to balance the federal budget or to streamline giant bureaucracies, can not be regarded as a serious substitute for economic planning. They simply suggest that our concern is to up-grade the procedures of administrative tinkering or to rearrange the marginal concessions that have been offered to rival groups—but not to tackle the grave difficulties now facing the U.S. economy. The consequences are predictable. Attempts to formulate an orderly allocation of investment funds or of human resources remain stifled by the fear that market forces will undermine any of the designs that can be devised. If the refusal to conceive of alternative visions and designs persists, we will condemn the exercise of economic planning to political futility before it can move into a higher gear.

The unreality of the debate over planning procedures is deeply cherished in a status quo society. Rejecting as utopian radicalism any reform that might offend our brokerage arrangements, we hold that strong profits make for good politics and a sound measure of the public interest. It must therefore be assumed that better procedures in group bargaining will lead to improved ratios of capital productivity, social investment returns, and business efficiency. We posit, too, that sophisticated measures of systems engineering are more important than new definitions of social purpose or political equality. It is in this light that technocratic planners debate the "public interest" as if it were the bottom line of an apolitical business entity whose life span is mythically endless.

APPENDIX
LIST OF
CONFERENCE PARTICIPANTS

Glen Cove, Long Island; October, 1976

DAVID E. APTER, Professor of Political Science, Yale University.

WILLIAM W. BETTERIDGE, Assistant Vice President, Rate and Tariff Planning, Administration C Department, AT&T.

GORDON T. BOWDEN, Director of Educational Relations, Public Relations and Employee Information Department, AT&T.

EDWARD S. GILL, Vice President, Corporate Planning, Bell Telephone Company of Pennsylvania.

ROBERT G. GILPIN, JR., Professor of Politics and International Affairs, Princeton University.

ELI GINZBERG, A. Barton Hepburn Professor of Economics, Columbia University; Director of the Conservation of Human Resources Project and Chairman, National Commission for Manpower Policy.

WALTER GOLDSTEIN, Professor of Political Science, State University of New York, Albany; Chairman, University Seminar on Technology and Social Change, Columbia.

ANDREW HACKER, Professor of Political Science, Queens College, City University of New York.

SYLVIA ANN HEWLETT, Assistant Professor of Economics, Barnard College and Columbia University.

DONALD U. HONICKY, Manager of College Relations, Public Relations and Employee Information Department, AT&T.

CARL E. HORN, Assistant Vice President, State Regulatory Activity, Division of State Regulatory Matters Department, AT&T.

JOHN A. KOTEN, Vice President, Public Relations, New Jersey Bell Telephone Company.

ROBERT LEKACHMAN, Distinguished Professor of Economics, Lehman College, City University of New York.

FRANKLIN A. LONG, Henry R. Luce Professor of Science and Society, and Professor of Chemistry, Cornell University.

A. H. MCKEAGE, Director of Tariffs and Costs, AT&T.

JOSEPH S. MURPHY, President, Queens College, 1970–1976; President, Bennington College, 1977–.

DEAN G. OSTRUM, Vice President, Regulatory Matters, Western Electric Company.

JAMES V. RYAN, Assistant Vice President, Public Relations and Employee Information Department, AT&T.

MARIO G. SALVADORI, Professor of Architecture, Emeritus, Columbia University.

ROSALIND S. SENECA, Assistant Professor of Economics, Columbia University.

RAYMOND VERNON, Herbert F. Johnson Professor of International Business Management, Graduate School of Business Administration; Director of the Center for International Affairs, Harvard University.

AARON W. WARNER, Director, University Seminars, and Dean, Continuing Education and Special Programs, Columbia University.

MURRAY L. WEIDENBAUM, Director of the Center for the Study of American Business and Mallinckrodt Distinguished University Professor, Washington University, St. Louis, Missouri.

RICHARD H. WILSON, Assistant Vice President, Service Costs, AT&T.

JOHN YINGLING, Director of Corporate Planning, AT&T.